"The [...] as documented at sacred sites are clues to an underlying reality of which few civilized people are aware."

— Dennis William Hauck
author of the *National Directory of Haunted Places*

Stroll through a forest of the world's oldest living trees, explore secret healing caves, or take a midnight dip in the hallowed waters of Big Sur! *Sacred Sites of the West* takes you on an exciting journey of enchantment and explains how the earth's energies can heal you, rejuvenate your inner energies, and affect your dreams. Investigate ley lines and grid networks, vortexes, and energy wellsprings—all here in the United States! Visit the "Lourdes of America" in New Mexico, tour the inner temple of a Hawaiian *heiau*, then raft the most treacherous rapids on the North American continent. See the never-before-documented Albino Redwood of California and the Child Nest Rock of Nevada. Dream spots, healing centers, goddess and warrior sites, temples, and vision caves are just a few of the places you'll encounter. Plus, color photographs, holy history, earth physics, and legends become an integral part of each site description, leaving you with a clear understanding of just what makes these sites so precious.

D0057674

About the Author

Bernyce Barlow is a retired educator and abuse therapist whose research and understanding of sacred site phenomena has helped hundreds of children and adults for over a decade.

Her on- and off-site seminars, classroom presentations, and enrichment programs have been accepted by the State of California and adopted by many placement facilities throughout the West.

Exposed to extensive travel throughout her life, Bernyce brings with her an attitude of familiarity and an unconditional acceptance toward sacred site research, as well as a woman's perspective of the energies to be found therein.

Bernyce bridges the gap between faith and physics, allowing readers to travel between the two, with an endearing approach that puts people at ease and in control. Her insights, charisma, and earthy sense of humor have helped her to become one of the most sought-out speakers in the West.

To Write to the Author

If you wish to contact the author or would like more information about this book, please write to the author in care of Llewellyn Worldwide, and we will forward your request. Both the author and publisher appreciate hearing from you and learning of your enjoyment of this book and how it has helped you. Llewellyn Worldwide cannot guarantee that every letter written to the author can be answered, but all will be forwarded. Please write to:

Llewellyn Worldwide Ltd.
P.O. Box 64383, Dept. K056-6, St. Paul, MN 55164-0383, U.S.A.
Please enclose a self-addressed, stamped envelope for reply, or $1.00 to cover costs. If outside U.S.A., enclose international postal reply coupon.

Free Catalog from Llewellyn

For more than ninety years Llewellyn has brought its readers knowledge in the fields of metaphysics and human potential. Learn about the newest books in spiritual guidance, natural healing, astrology, occult philosophy, and more. Enjoy book reviews, New Age articles, a calendar of events, plus current advertised products and services. To get your free copy of *Llewellyn's New Worlds*, send your name and address to:

Llewellyn's New Worlds of Mind and Spirit
P.O. Box 64383, Dept. K056-6, St. Paul, MN 55164-0383, U.S.A.

SACRED SITES
OF THE WEST

BERNYCE BARLOW

BOULDER CITY LIBRARY
813 ARIZONA STREET
BOULDER CITY, NV 89005-2697

FEB   1998

1996
Llewellyn Publications
St. Paul, Minnesota, 55164-0383, U.S.A.

Sacred Sites of the West. Copyright © 1996 by Bernyce Barlow. All rights reserved. Printed in the United States of America. No part of this book may be used or reproduced in any manner whatsoever without written permission from Llewellyn Publications, except in the case of brief quotations embodied in critical articles or reviews.

FIRST EDITION
First Printing, 1996

Cover Photography by Cheyenne Rousse
Cover Photography, petroglyphs, by Stephen Dombrosk
Cover Design by Maria Mazzara
Editing and Interior Design by Connie Hill

Library of Congress Cataloging-in-Publication Data
Barlow, Bernyce, 1951–
    Sacred sites of the west / Bernyce Barlow.
        p.   cm. —
    Includes bibliographical references (p.   ) and index.
        ISBN 1-56718-056-6 (trade pbk.)
        1. West (U.S.) — Guidebooks. 2. Sacred space — West (U.S.) —
Guidebooks. 3. West (U.S.) — Description and travel. I. Title.
    F590.3.B37   1996
    291.3'5'0978—dc20 96-28359
                                                                      CIP

Llewellyn Publications
A Division of Llewellyn Worldwide, Ltd.
St. Paul, Minnesota 55164-0383, U.S.A.

Table of Contents

The Goddess

The Warrior

Sacred Mountains, Sacred Trees

Observation

Sacred Sites of the West Maps

List of Map Sites

1. Iao Valley, Maui, Hawaii
2. Haleakala, Maui, Hawaii
3. Mo'okini, Hawaii
4. Hill of the Whale, Hawaii
5. Petroglyph Field, Hawaii
6. City of Refuge, Hawaii
7. Kilauea Caldera, Hawaii
8. Mauna Loa, Hawaii
9. Catalina Island, California
10. Point Conception, California
11. Coastal Dream Caves, California
12. Mount San Antonio (Mount Baldy), California
13. The Lavenderia at San Luis Rey Mission, California
14. Indian Canyons, Palm Springs, California
15. Joshua Tree National Forest, California
16. Blyth Intaglios, California
17. Death Valley, California
18. Panamint Intaglios, California
19. Bristlecone Forest, California
20. Big Sur, California
21. Albino Redwoods, California
22. Santa Cruz Magnetic Fields, California
23. Mount Diablo, California
24. Mount Tamalpias, California
25. Dense Redwood Groves, California
26. Fern Canyon, California
27. Shasta Caverns, California
28. Burney Falls, California
29. Mount Shasta, California
30. Jedidiah Smith State Park, California
31. Gold Beach Magnetic Fields, Oregon
32. Crater Lake, Oregon
33. Mount Hood, Oregon
34. Mount St. Helens, Washington

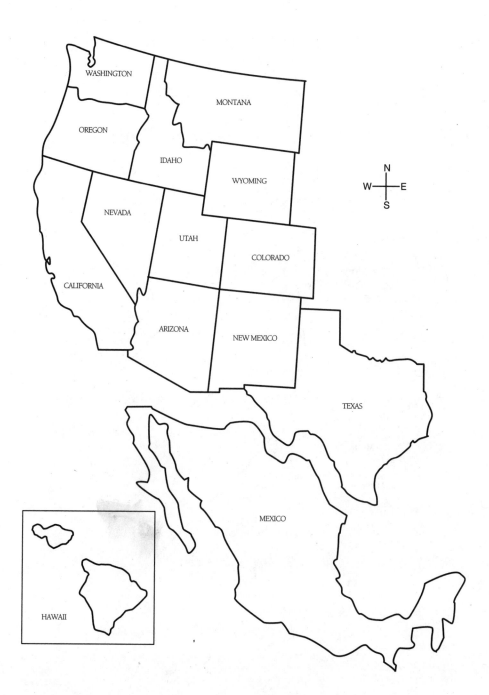

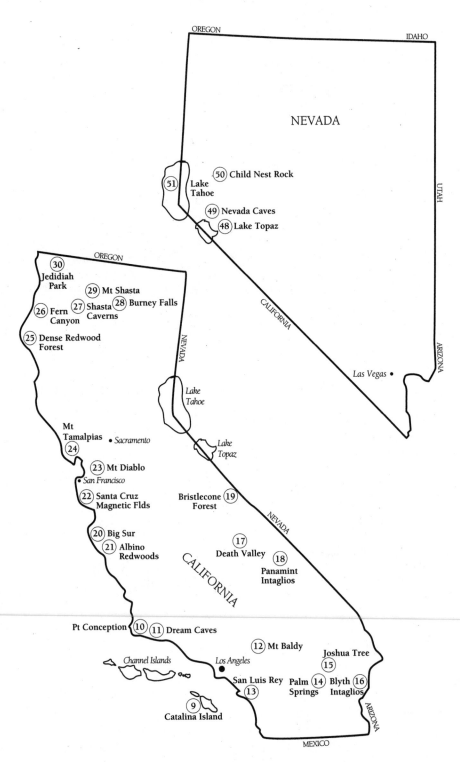

NEVADA

OREGON
IDAHO

UTAH

(50) Child Nest Rock

(51) Lake
Tahoe

(49) Nevada Caves
(48) Lake Topaz

CALIFORNIA

ARIZONA

Las Vegas •

OREGON

(30)
Jedidiah
Park

(29) Mt Shasta

(26) Fern (27) Shasta (28) Burney Falls
Canyon Caverns

(25) Dense Redwood
Forest

NEVADA

Lake
Tahoe

Mt
Tamalpias • Sacramento
(24)

Lake
Topaz

(23) Mt Diablo
• San Francisco

(22) Santa Cruz
Magnetic Flds

Bristlecone (19)
Forest

NEVADA

(20) Big Sur
(21) Albino
Redwoods

CALIFORNIA

(17)
Death Valley
(18)
Panamint
Intaglios

Pt Conception (10)(11) Dream Caves

(12) Mt Baldy
Joshua Tree
Channel Islands Los Angeles •
(15)

San Luis Rey Palm (14) Blyth (16)
(13) Springs Intaglios

ARIZONA

(9)
Catalina Island

MEXICO

X

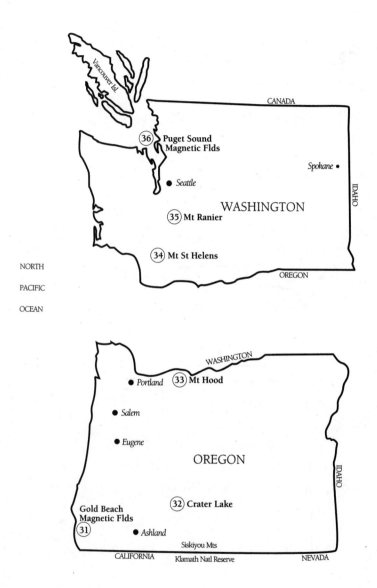

CANADA

Vancouver Isl.

36 **Puget Sound Magnetic Flds**

Spokane ●

IDAHO

● *Seattle*

WASHINGTON

35 **Mt Ranier**

34 **Mt St Helens**

NORTH

PACIFIC

OCEAN

OREGON

WASHINGTON

● *Portland*   33 **Mt Hood**

● *Salem*

● *Eugene*

OREGON

IDAHO

32 **Crater Lake**

Gold Beach Magnetic Flds

31   ● *Ashland*

Siskiyou Mts

CALIFORNIA   Klamath Natl Reserve   NEVADA

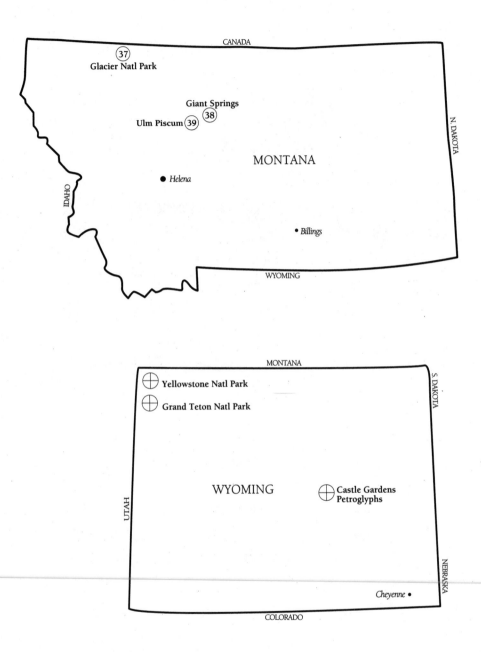

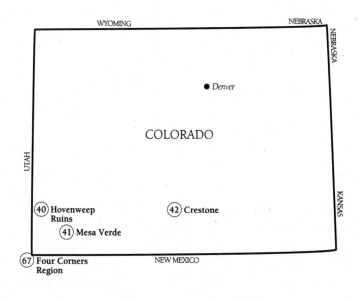

WYOMING NEBRASKA

NEBRASKA

● *Denver*

COLORADO

UTAH

40 Hovenweep Ruins
42 Crestone

41 Mesa Verde

KANSAS

67 Four Corners Region

NEW MEXICO

67 Four Corners Region

COLORADO

OKLAHOMA

71 Taos

69 Chaco Canyon Natl Mon.
70 Chimayo
● *Santa Fe*

Sangre de Cristo Mtns

ARIZONA

● *Albuquerque*

NEW MEXICO

● *Roswell*

TEXAS

TEXAS

MEXICO

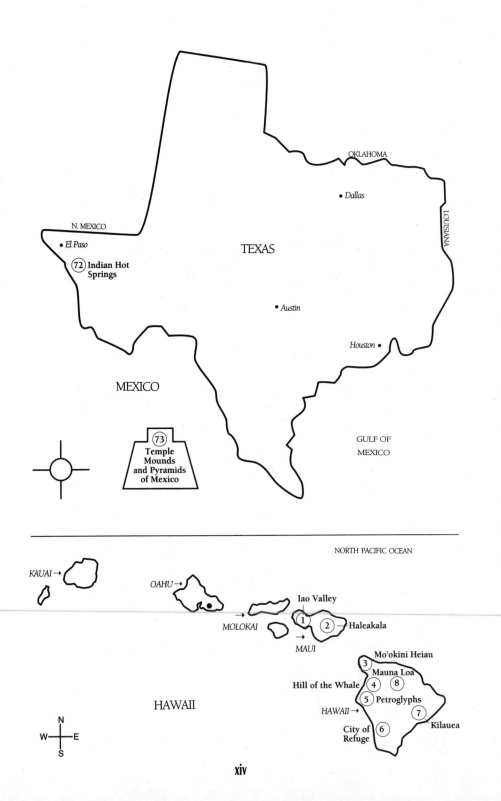

OKLAHOMA

• Dallas

LOUISIANA

N. MEXICO

• El Paso

TEXAS

(72) Indian Hot
Springs

• Austin

Houston •

MEXICO

GULF OF
MEXICO

(73)
Temple
Mounds
and Pyramids
of Mexico

NORTH PACIFIC OCEAN

KAUAI →

OAHU →

Iao Valley

(1)

MOLOKAI →

(2) — Haleakala

MAUI →

Mo'okini Heiau

(3)

Mauna Loa

Hill of the Whale

(4) (8)

(5) Petroglyphs

HAWAII →

(7)

HAWAII

Kilauea

City of
Refuge

(6)

N
W — E
S

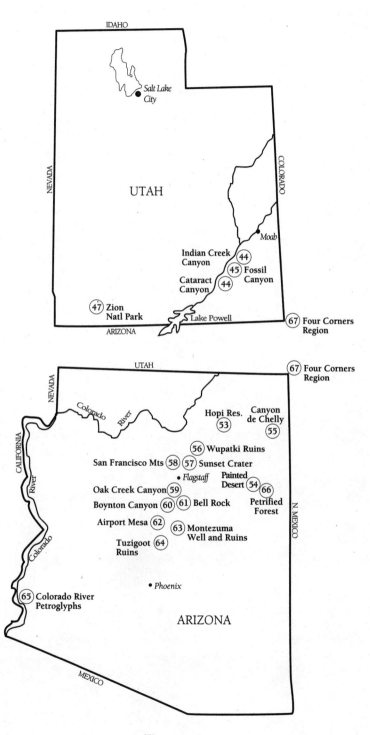

IDAHO

Salt Lake City

NEVADA

UTAH

COLORADO

Moab

Indian Creek Canyon (44)

(45) Fossil Canyon

Cataract Canyon (44)

(47) Zion Natl Park

Lake Powell

(67) Four Corners Region

ARIZONA

UTAH

(67) Four Corners Region

NEVADA

Colorado River

Hopi Res. (53)

Canyon de Chelly (55)

CALIFORNIA

(56) Wupatki Ruins

San Francisco Mts (58) (57) Sunset Crater

• Flagstaff

Painted Desert (54) (66)

Oak Creek Canyon (59)

Boynton Canyon (60) (61) Bell Rock

Petrified Forest

River

Airport Mesa (62)

(63) Montezuma Well and Ruins

N. MEXICO

Tuzigoot Ruins (64)

Colorado

• Phoenix

(65) Colorado River Petroglyphs

ARIZONA

MEXICO

GAIA

CHAPTER 1

EARTH PHYSICS

Each one of us comes from a culture that at one time was acutely aware of the wonders of the earth. Every nook and cranny of the planet once hosted a people whose life depended in part on their relationship with their environment. As we race toward the twenty-first century, we again find ourselves in the same position as our ancestors, dependent on the earth for survival. For many years the earth was stripped of her resources wantonly, as if there were no end to them. There seemed to be no conscience within industry, business, or science. But as plants, animals, and ocean life became extinct we saw there was indeed an end, and that our attitude had to change, as a planet, about the planet. That is where we stand today, within the change of consciousness toward the earth, a consciousness common to all through a shared ancestral gene pool deeply rooted in the wisdom of the ages.

Part of this wisdom was centered around the recognition and utilization of "places of power," or what is popularly called a sacred site in today's terminology. What distinguishes a sacred site as special (as opposed to somewhere else twenty miles down the road that may be just as beautiful or endearing) is the unique combination of energies that collect there. Often these energies are present due to geo-anomalies within the earth's vast telluric system that have found their way to the surface. Other times the energy is created from imprint residue left from generations of history or struggle. The personality of that struggle may be felt at a site even if it occurred decades or centuries before.[1] An oddity? Yes, but nevertheless all too true. Consider places like the City of Refuge in Hawaii, Little Big Horn, or some of the Civil War battlefields. Even if there was not a speck of anomalous energy near these places, the psychic imprint would be strong enough to mark the site as special due to the ambiance created through its holy history. But I am getting ahead of myself here, so first let's back up a bit to take a look at the big picture, the masterpiece called Gaia. After that we will focus on specifics.

In order to personalize the planet in the mid-1970s, living earth theorists named her Gaia, after the Greek earth goddess. The entire living earth movement was focused on the concept that the planet was in fact alive and these activists went about using scientific methods to prove their point.[2] The idea of a living planet was not at all foreign to the global population until the 1500s when science began to evolve. That evolution took us down a path leading as far away from the living earth concept as possible. It somehow seems right that science is now playing a major role in reversing this trend.

Although there are many facets to the living earth theory, it is held together with a kind of cosmic glue that has its own consciousness. This cohesive consciousness is based on the premise that living organisms (right down to the string) have the ability to intentionally organize the elements of the universe into life-expressing components (asparagus, people, rocks, etc.) through energy-signal frequencies that all living things emit. In science this is a prerequisite to qualify as a living thing. Homeostasis, the ability to self-regulate, is also a part of the Gaian theory, because energy must have the ability to self-regulate in order to be classified as living. If Einstein is correct, then all matter is condensed energy where life-force frequencies are not lost in the metamorphosis from one form to another. If we accept the overwhelming scientific information that has been put together over the last fifty years, there is a very strong argument for the Earth as a living organism, especially after taking into consideration that Gaia emits energy-signal frequencies at the most miniscule cellular levels which are responsible for the processes of organization and homeostasis on the planet. If we commit ourselves to the realization that Gaia is a living conscious organism that creates the very energy fields that we depend on to exist (through a very complex network of signal communications and natural laws), a partnership will naturally develop between the earth and her inhabitants based on survival, mutual respect, and knowledge.

Pioneer biologist Rupert Sheldrake suggested there were certain energy fields that did not follow the rules of physics because these fields were made up of neither energy nor matter. To shake things up even more, Sheldrake suggested the morphic resonance these fields produce develops and organizes energy into matter through some sort of ethereal genetic code that has been developed through the ages.

This formative causation is based on the principle that if something has been done, even once, the knowledge of how to do that something again is recorded and available through the morphogenetic field. This knowledge can be channeled through all living things, energy, or matter, at the most diminutive level of physics. The bottom line is that the morphogenetic field is also available for us to tap into. Even if you are doing something for the first time, if it has been done before, it has been recorded within the field, and the knowledge is accessible. The more something has been repeated, the stronger that code is within the field. If you are seeking answers to questions that have already been answered, the knowledge is available.

By now you may be wondering why I have chosen to introduce the sacred sites via life-force dynamism. It is because these forces are an integral part of these centers. Their condensed energies affect us right down to the marrow in our bones—conscious cellular interaction with the earth, what a great concept! Even though the types of frequencies at the sites vary, the common bond is that they are clearly distinct and have the ability to influence us on a number of levels: spiritually, mentally, and physically. This is because we are made up of the same components as the rest of the universe, just arranged differently. The life force energies found at these power spots seem to act as a bridge between conscious energy and conscious matter. Of course, what that bridge connects each of us to is strictly a personal matter.

Energy was given a bum rap in the first part of the century, except by Einstein. It was assigned three forms: gas, liquid, solid. As technology progressed, other types of energy of different consistencies were added to the list. For instance, plasma and bioplasma are states of condensed energy, conduits of "energy consciousness" that are admittedly elusive, but definitely there and measurable. The nightly plasma light show seen from Mafta, Texas, is a good example of the existence of plasma fields and their effects. What makes plasma fields so unique is that the atoms within the field are not fully developed; instead electrons and other types of highly charged subatomic matter bounce off each other, causing spectacular light shows like the aurora borealis.

Biofields are not as easy to identify. You usually need a clue to help you find them. Fortunately, we have been given more than just a clue to where these anomalies can be found. We know where they are located, as well as their history and cultural significance, because they have already been identified as sacred sites centuries earlier by the indigenous People. Although some sites remain unknown to the public, many others are protected within state or federal monuments, national forests, or by private conservatories. I do not mean to imply that the government is protecting biofields intentionally; they are not. It just so happens that biofields exist in the places we consider special enough to protect.

Dennis William Hauck, paranormal researcher, media consultant, and author of a number of books including *The National Directory of Haunted Places,* describes the biofield and what it does this way, "There are places like Canyon de Chelly, Bandalero, and Chaco Canyon, Native American sites where people constantly report sightings of a ghost-like nature. These places are referred to as sacred sites. There is something about the biofield in these places that allows certain dimensions of energy to partially materialize, become condensed. That is the reason that the spirit of place can materialize itself into what is called the *genis loci,* or local spirit."[3]

Mr. Hauck also adds, "There are places where the energies are not positive. I believe this has to do with an imprint or a group of imprints left behind that somehow convey a malevolent feeling. You feel this at places where tragic occurrences have happened. I can not say exactly why but paranormal experiences seem to happen in areas where the energy has condensed allowing some form or another of manifestation." $E=MC^2$!

As we leave the subject of matter/energy anomalies to explore other factors involved with sacred sites, keep in mind we are not leaving behind the concept of energy per se, but one type of energy (called prana, chi, biofield, orgone, or life force) that somehow becomes amplified enough at sacred sites to communicate with other life forms. Enough for now on biofields, except to say the energy produced from these fields often develops and enhances the "spirit of place" at a site.

Spirit of place is a term often used in conjunction with sacred sites. It is a word that characterizes the personality or ambiance of a site. It is more than a materialized apparition, it is the purpose of the site embodied through spirituality. Sometimes a spirit of place is bold and dynamic, as is Pele from the Hawaiian Islands. Seen as an old lady, a

Photo by Berryce Barlow

New earth, less than an hour old, shines like silver in the Pacific sunlight. The spirit of Pele is always evolving.

young woman, a traveler in a red dress, or a white dog, Pele takes on many forms, but none are as impressive as the violent temper tantrums when she hurls from her caldera molten rocks, gasses, and glowing debris. True, it is the geophysical strata beneath the island of Hawaii that is the direct cause of all this havoc, but through centuries of legends, religious beliefs, and cultural traditions (including human sacrifice to appease this feisty goddess), the spirit of Pele is very much alive.

Not all spirits of place are so antagonistic. The quaint adobe chapel called the "Lourdes of America" found in Chimayo, New Mexico, is said to have a spirit of place that is loving, healing, and disposed to miracles. Father Migel Mateo of the Santuario of Chimayo feels the answer to the mysteries of Chimayo "lies in the faith of those that come to the chapel to be healed" and quickly adds, "all things are possible with Christ." Father Mateo's promised prayers for this project were an inspiration to me. In response to my request to sum up the power of Chimayo, he wrote: "Very simply, the consistent faith in God of people who come to pray at El Santuario de Chimayo is what Santuario de Chimayo is all about. Nothing else."[4]

As we delve deeper into the psyche of the sacred sites, we find there is more than meets the eye. We know energies on a cellular level connect us with the earth's consciousness. We also know there are spiritual characteristics imbued in the land that manifest themselves in a myriad of ways as the spirit of place. What we don't know is how these energies affect us in other dimensions—nor do we know that much about other dimensions, except that they are there and we can tap into them under certain conditions, such as those found at vortex sites.

Just as artesian water wells and springs break through to the earth's surface via underground fissures and cracks, there are also places where telluric energies break through in a similar fashion. These sites are popularly called energy wellsprings and vortexes, and are considered holy ground. Vortexes affect us dramatically. All kinds of things happen at vortex sites because of the deeper levels of bio-energy they affect. Sedona, Arizona and Mount Shasta, California are two very well-known vortex sites that have been considered sacred since prehistoric times.

Biochemist/brain scientist, Pete Sanders, author of *You Are Psychic!*, helps us in his book to understand what is going on at vortex sites by unraveling the mystery behind the "string theory." Sanders writes, "Subatomic physicists are always trying to find the smallest bit of

Photo by Bernyce Barlow

Airport Mesa, Sedona, Arizona. Note the sparse vegetation, an indication of electrical vortexes. This site generates an energized charge that is considered a balanced electrical vortex.

"stuff" that makes up all things. They feel they've identified it, and they call that smallest bit a string. They picked a common name like string instead of "quark" or "neutrino" or "pi meson" because these strings literally tie together all the forces, energies, and theories of the universe. If you twist them one way, these strings will become a proton; twist them another way and they will become an electron; twist them still a different way and they become a photon of light; twist them still another way and they become a graviton, the mysterious particle or force that makes gravity work."

With a progressive spirit (and no doubt a twinkle in his eye) the M.I.T.-trained scientist goes on to say: "that the top physicists around the world, [from] M.I.T., Princeton, Cal-Tech, Berkeley, Oxford, Germany, Russia—all agree that these strings exist in ten dimensions. Three of space, one of time, and then they say very rapidly, and-six-other-dimensions-we-don't-have-the-technology-to-measure-yet. For the first time, the top scientists around the world are admitting that there are dimensions beyond that we don't have a clue how to measure technologically." Sanders concludes, "What is happening at the vortex sites is energy flow in those deeper dimensions."[5]

If you hang around vortex sites for a while, you hear all kinds of experiences that range from the paranormal to achieving deeply spiritual states—not surprising, considering that the energy flows at vortexes exist in dimensions deeper than those we encounter on a day to day basis. For some, these energies have been life changing! The vortex process is a part of the earth's homeostasis system, where Gaia not only heals herself, but us as well!

If we look at the earth as a whole, what we will find is a system that, left undisturbed, has intelligent purpose and intent. Not to have this knowledge or to ignore it creates an unhealthy attitude and atmosphere toward the planet. Not until we look at Gaia as a living organism will we see her destiny—a destiny that includes us, for better or worse. The sacred sites on Earth are places where we can clearly experience the existing power behind the inspiration of creation—through the union of compatible amplified energies that trigger higher levels of awareness, states of consciousness, and healing. As we further explore these energies, keep in mind the spirit of place at the sacred sites is as individual and diverse in purpose as those who live on the planet, acting out their own personality and character through will and (predestined?) choice. Now, more about Earth energies!

CHAPTER 2

AIR IONS

Everywhere around us are "unseen influences." We know that they are there and often how they operate. When we watch a magnet tug on a metal paper clip, we know we are watching an unseen force in action. There are many such forces interacting on this planet, laws of physics that govern the bumping and grinding, whirling and swirling of atomic and sub-atomic particles that often interact seemingly as invisible agents. Most folks have never seen an electron or photon—we know they are there because science has told us about them.

This chapter is about one of those invisible forces that we cannot see but are dramatically affected by: air ions. An ion can be simply defined as an atom or group of atoms that display an excess or a deficiency of electrons. An atom that loses an electron forms a cation or a positively charged ion.[1] An atom that gains an electron becomes an anion or negatively charged ion. Atoms can be converted to ions by a myriad of radionic activities such as X-rays, light, or energy. When something is ionized, the molecules of the substance separate and do not share equal electrons, making them positive or negative in charge. The Laws of Faraday were based on ionization. Geo-anomalies at sacred sites, such as Rollright, England, have been found to harbor areas that act as Faraday cages, blocking certain types of radionic waves![2]

The Earth creates both positive and negative air ions in a number of ways. A comfortable balance for Gaia is a ratio of four to five, balanced on either end positively or negatively. In places like the San Gabriel Valley in Southern California, the scales have tipped way off, showing numbers like thirty-three positive air ions to two negative. Any time there is an abundance of positive ions in the atmosphere the effects are detrimental. When anything in nature gets tipped over, someone gets hurt—unfortunately, the San Gabriel Valley is feeling the bruising of ionic abuse.

Positive ions are generated in a number of ways, not only through natural causes but also by humans. The warm winds that blow around our planet are one source that creates positive ions. In Washington State these snow melting winds are called the Chinook, and in Southern California these gusts are referred to as the Santa Ana winds.[3] All over the planet indigenous people refer to these winds as harbingers of ill will, or the dark witches' winds. In some countries, if a crime of passion is committed during these winds, the sentence may be reduced due to the age-old observation that at times the witches' winds make folks a little crazy! Actually, it is not the winds that set people off, it is the copious amount of positive ions they generate. Too many positive ions in the atmosphere and people get edgy, sluggish, and depressed, due to the neurological changes caused by the ions.[4] That is why in nature there are more available negative ion sources than positive ion sources.

Positive ions are also created by environmental pollutants, forced air systems, exhaust fumes, and layers of smog. When the mind, body, and spirit have to operate under such stress as mega doses of positive ionized air particles, especially in closed conditions, something has to give, and it is usually a sacrifice of one of the above or all three. Positive ions are a natural part of Gaia's environmental check and balance system. When left alone the planet self-regulates this system to our benefit—altered and unchecked it harms us.

Negative ions, on the other hand, are nature's caress, calming and soothing, unlike their door-slamming counterpart. More often than not sacred sites register a high count of free-flowing negative air ions. Negative ions are created by some of the most awesome, beautiful, and powerful forces in nature like waterfalls, rivers, minerals, storms, forests, blowholes, subterranean water routes, uranium-rich earth, and crashing waves. Negative air ions are created where the earth plays! When combined with other geo-influences, like the energy patterns

Photo by Deb Olson

Desert and ocean blowholes are among the phenomena that create negative air ions, as water-cooled air is forced to the surface. La Buffadora in Baja, Mexico is an excellent example of a West Coast ocean blowhole.

from vortexes or grid networks, ecstacy experiences flow as freely as the ions themselves.

This occurence has an explanation—it is a simple case of physics effecting human neurology. How neurotransmitters are affected by ions is not quite as simple to explain. People have devoted entire lifetimes to researching this field of study and the verdict is not yet in. However, what is known is that the flow of a neurotransmitter called serotonin[5] (the chairman of the board of neurotransmitters) is deregulated when exposed to an abundance of negative ions. The effect of that deregulation manifests itself in a number of different ways. People under the influence of this anomaly find themselves more receptive creatively and spiritually. In order to listen we must be able to hear. Negative ion-influenced sites have the uncanny ability to quiet a busy mind.

Another benefit to negative ion fields is the capability they possess to enhance relaxation, meditation, visualization, and guided imagery. Again, this is a direct result of deregulated serotonin. At its most extreme, serotonin can be completely blocked, as it is with LSD, the hallucinogenic drug of the 1960s. When this happens, messages sent to the brain run helter-skelter, trying to find new pathways via unfamiliar

Photo by Bernyce Barlow

In the Badlands of North Dakota, uranium-rich rock and soil generate negative ions, encouraging a serene state of body, mind, and soul.

neurotransmitter agents and routes generally reserved for other functions. The results manifest in altered perceptions, sometimes at a higher level of consciousness, sometimes not—but always in a manner that is foreign to the conscious, like out of control hallucinations.

Unlike chemical serotonin blockers, negative ions are not extreme in their influence. They open the door to a more serene state that is gentle on the mind, body, and soul, where perceptions are allowed to wander within the safe boundaries the conscious understands and can integrate. This allows you to control your experience on a physical level without losing touch with the spiritual dimensions where healing, knowledge, and empowerment originate. Once this door is open, the ability to understand the higher levels of consciousness within ourselves is enhanced and the beauty comes dancing out.

Someone who truly understands this concept is Dr. Jean Quinn, Ph.D., who holds degrees from Stanford University, Pacific Oaks College, Cal State Los Angeles, and Claremont Graduate School. She has been involved actively with teaching, administrating, and helping to formulate laws that have protected the challenged learning field for the past forty years. Dr. Quinn's accomplishments are indeed impressive, but equally impressive is her ability to integrate meditation, visualization, guided imagery, and healing into growth stepping stones toward wellness. Her reputation as one of the most dynamic pioneers of her time is deserved and well earned.

It was Dr. Quinn who impressed upon me how important the skills of meditation, guided imagery, and visualization are in daily life. In the classroom, Quinn taught these skills along with math and reading. A negative ion machine was in the classroom as an educational tool next to the textbooks and the classroom pet. Eventually, Dr. Quinn's learning-challenged students recognized the road to healing and education because they could see it in their precious imaginations.[6] Most went on successfully from there. As for my contribution to Dr. Quinn's classroom? Instead of bringing the negative ion generator to the students, I brought the students to the generator, Gaia herself, which I consider the ideal classroom for both gifted and learning-challenged students in which to learn the sciences.

Meditation, visualization, and guided imagery are not just for entertainment, but can enhance creativity, spiritual sensitivity, self-examination, healing, learning, and educating. What negative ions do is turbo-boost these skills. This is why it is most important to protect the natural resources on this planet that generate these little ionic wonders of wellness. Although negative ions are an invisible influence, they are a powerful one. Given the chance, their effect is like a kiss from Gaia that can spark the imagination and ignite the soul.

Negative ions and sacred sites go hand in hand, whether the site is a healing site, a renewal site, or a dreaming site. What enchants me the most is the diversity of ionic sites. They can be found everywhere! In the desolate Four Corners region (of Arizona, New Mexico, Utah, and Colorado) labyrinths of underground caverns carry water and air beneath the parched desert floor.[7] Occasionally, what is called a blowhole appears, an opening in the earth where the water-cooled air rushes out when the air pressure below ground is greater than above ground. The opposite pressure causes the reverse to happen and air is sucked in.[8] These blowholes have been heard twenty miles away, and have been clocked at thirty miles per hour, under specific circumstances. The air that rushes out from these blowholes is made up of an abundance of negative ions (keep in mind the earth around the Four Corners area is rich in uranium and, in places, iron). The sounds made by these blowholes exhibit combined forces that generate negative ions from more than just one source, making these sites extremely powerful. There are many Native American stories about the blowholes, not only emergence stories, but legends that tell of the sites' ability to trigger altered states. An accessible blowhole is found at Wupatki, Arizona.

Photo by Tom Snyder

Burney Falls combines environmental and telluric energy forces that can inspire a transcendental experience. Nearby, the active volcano, Mount Lassen, bubbles and steams, adding to the regional physics.

Another site with a high-ion count is Burney Falls in Northern California. Although it is different in geological appearance, it is just as potent. At Burney you will again be looking at combined forces at work, some telluric and others that are environmental. The massive volume of water that throws itself into the green pools beside the volcanic cliffs generates more than enough energy by itself to trigger a transcendental experience, but when combined with the volcanic energy/nature of the land, the forests, the river, and the wind, an ecstacy wonderland is created for the psyche to run through.

In your journeys, keep a watch out for the sacred places that generate negative ions. Keep them safe. Know that where there is an ocean, a waterfall, or a river, there is also healing. Seek out these centers and give them a chance to integrate with your personality. It is a good way to introduce yourself to Gaia and a perfect opportunity for Gaia to introduce herself to you.

CHAPTER 3

LEY LINES AND GRID NETS

The grid net/ley line system has been compared to the acupuncture meridians of the human body—they simply follow a grid course. Grids and leys are part of a network of channels that send and receive energies that encompass the globe. The type of energy fields at any given point differs, depending on the character of the field.

For instance, the three most recognized grid networks are the Curry net, the Hartman net, and the controversial Cathie net. Each has its own distinct pattern. The Curry net has a regulated energy system running from southwest to northeast and is affected by radiation, the rotation of the Earth, and magnetism.[1] The Hartman net displays phase changes every six hours, and is not as stable as the Curry grid because of its sensitivity to sunspots, meteorological conditions, and moon phases. The Hartman grid runs from north to south and east to west.

Then there is the Cathie net, discovered by a man in New Zealand who claims the net is a grid of rectangles, each forty-five square nautical miles in distance, that are affected by gravity, the speed of light, and the mass of the earth.[2] UFO buffs say the Cathie grid attracts crafts who appear to use the network's energy field.

A more down-to-earth use of the grid net system can be seen in the migratory patterns of birds, fish, and animals who follow these energy paths in order to continue the survival of their species. It is no mystery

Photo by Bernyce Barlow

"As it is above, so it is below"; lightning strikes seek out grids and leys near the Rio Grande, New Mexico. The Rio Grande plateau receives more lightning strikes than anywhere else in the United States.

how the swallows find their way each year to the grounds of Mission San Juan Capistrano. They simply follow a grid course.

Ley lines are structured differently than grid nets. They do not follow the same geometrical rules that grids do. This does not mean they are spread willy-nilly across the planet. They are not, but their nomenclature is not as easily recognized as a grid net. They are more like telluric pathways. In the early 1920s, an English merchant, Alfred Watkins, coined the phrase "straight tracks" during his research on ley lines. He mapped leys throughout England, and found that they appeared to connect one holy shrine with another.[3] Closer inspection of Watkins' survey showed a certain correlation between sacred sites and straight tracks, although some of Watkins' tracks appeared to be coincidental or wishful thinking. There was enough evidence to prove some facts underlining his theory but it would be some years before the mysteries of Watkins' straight tracks would be unraveled.

Watkins' observations would certainly not have been anything new to our ancient ancestors. They knew all about the ley line paths and how they worked, as well as how to amplify them. In the outback of Australia, the Aborigines called the ley system a "line of songs." On the North American continent, the leys were known as "spirit paths."

How ley lines and grid nets affect us is extremely complex. There are as many different effects as there are meridians, although it can be generally said that certain patterns produce specific results. Not all energy patterns are good for us. Germany has been a forerunner in studying how the energies of their regional grid system affects their citizens, and towns and facilities are being built accordingly.[4] The Chinese science of feng shui has been around for thousands of years, joining the dynamism of earth and man together in harmony. Feng shui recognizes too much yin energy is not healthy, nor is too much yang. The secret of balance comes with understanding the earth's energies.

In the western hemisphere, we speak in terms of magnetic and electrical energy, but this is no different than the yin and yang energy of our neighbors across the sea. Only the terms are different, the same rules still apply. For example, there are grids leys that display such a strong magnetic force that planes and boats need to adjust their compasses up to fifteen degrees to make up for the magnetic pull. A common complaint in a highly charged magnetic area is feeling sick to one's stomach or getting a headache. Obviously, this would not be an area where you would want to build a hospital or a facility whose instruments are sensitive to magnetic fields.

It is just as important to understand the beneficial side of leys and grids. The intersection points of grid nets can really kick out a tremendous force of energy. Sometimes this energy can produce some dramatic effects after interacting with human biochemistry, like heightened creativity, rejuvenation, healing, or enhanced spirituality. More often than not, grid intersections have been recognized and used for their specific qualities by ancient cultures who followed the ley paths to the sacred anomalies.

Grid networks and ley lines are a part of our lives, whether we are aware of them or not. They are an integral part of the global ecosystem. It seems senseless not to tap into and use the beneficial energies of these sites when they are so readily accessible to us. To acknowledge the unique energies found along the ley and grid network is a step well taken on a spirit path that can lead the traveler to a better understanding of the relationship we have with Gaia.

CHAPTER 4

VORTEXES

W hen it comes to vortexes, terminology appears to be the Achilles heel of the subject. Among folks pursuing this field, even the term "vortex" can stir up a lively conversation. Vortex is the popular term used to describe powerful energy patterns emitting from the earth. Imagine an artesian spring forcefully bubbling up from the ground. You can see the water emerging from the earth. An electric vortex is like an artesian spring, but instead of water coming from the site you get energy. Other vortexes are more like a vacuum than a spring and appear to draw energy into the earth. These vortexes are referred to as magnetic.

The terms "magnetic" and "electric" do not apply to the kind of energy found at a vortex, but to its effect. Electrical vortexes give you a charge. They are extremely energizing and lively, but they do not emit wellsprings of electricity as we know it. The same goes for magnetic vortexes. The term magnetic refers to the draw of the vortex, as a magnet draws metal. It does not mean there are great amounts of magnetic energy at the site. There are also lateral and electromagnetic vortexes whose energy patterns match their names.[1]

Scientists prefer to call vortex sites geophysical anomalies and have studied the effects of these sites on human behavior for some time. Native Americans have used vortex energy for thousands of years for a myriad of purposes. They considered vortexes holy and treated them as such.

The red rock canyonlands of Sedona, Arizona, host some of the most powerful vortex sites in the western United States. For reasons concerning cracks and fissures, faultlines, ley lines, grid intersections, underground rivers, high amounts of iron and magnesium in the soil, and a beauty of a negative ion count, Sedona has a personality all its own. There are a number of vortexes in this region and they interact with so many other kinds of earth energies that the vortex experience can become a mental barbell workout.

Before the Spanish arrived in the Via Verde Valley, pilgrimages were made to Sedona from as far north as Canada and as far south as Central America. The tremendous energies of the canyons were renowned throughout the western part of the continent. No one lived in the canyons; that would be sacrilege. They were reserved as a holy place for spiritual growth and knowledge.[2]

Sedona is a great example of a place to go if you really want to experience vortex energy, but it certainly is not the only place vortexes exist. On the contrary, some of the best-known sacred sites in the world

Photo by Bernyce Barlow

Canyonlands of Sedona, Arizona, viewed from Long Valley Mesa, where the Medicine Wheel shown on the cover is located. Pulsating forces generated from nearby Long, Red, Boynton, Secret, and Fay Canyons barrage this site with their combined energies.

Photo by Tom Snyder

Burney Falls, Mount Shasta, California creates a lateral energy pattern along Hat Creek. Lateral patterns promote a feeling of well-being and balance.

have been built on top of a vortex such as Stonehenge, England, or the Pyramid of Giza. Mount Shasta in Northern California and the City of Refuge on the island of Hawaii are also very powerful vortex sites.

People often ask what they should expect at a vortex. I hesitate to say. I will say that although experiences are as unique as the individuals having them, there is an overall common flavor that is shared at any given site. This is due to the character or spirit of place of the site. Spirit of place really sums up the purpose of an energy center. It is made up of the geophysics, the holy history, and the spirituality of the land. If a site is an electrical vortex center, you can be assured that you will feel energized. What you do with that energy is where the experience becomes individualized.

Just as ions, leys, and grids interact with human biochemistry, so do vortexes. As a therapist, I used vortex energy to stir up the subconscious in order to bring it to the conscious surface. Some vortexes amplify emotions. These sites were especially useful when I was working with sexually abused adolescents. I also used specific vortexes to polish up a mood or just to play in.

While exploring dream therapy with the kids, I found they dreamed like crazy at (magnetic) vortex sites that emitted morphogenic fields. Overnight campouts were often planned around these sites. I also used vortex energy patterns to settle a group down. There is a small magnetic vortex in San Dimas Canyon, California, where I did sessions with kids who were particularly angry or violent. It gave me the edge. I utilized electrical vortexes to soothe the incredible emotional pain these kids carried as well.[3]

After a decade of sacred site sessions with some of the most damaged children you will ever come across, I can honestly say the earth has the potential to emotionally and physically heal us through all kinds of channels. Vortexes are just one more tool for us to use in the search for healing.

CHAPTER 5

NATURAL PHENOMENA

G aia is full of surprises! In the Grand Canyon late one summer evening, I saw balls of light distribute electrical energy over an ionized mesa. It was a light show to beat all light shows, reminding me of the aurora borealis, another one of nature's spectacular sky shows. Glowing lights have also been seen over the Andes and in the swamp areas of the southern United States. Mount Shasta, California, has its fair share of natural light phenomena as well.

Anywhere you have combined energy fields, there is a chance you will see some sort of effect. Lightning is a great example. There are approximately 6,000 flashes of lightning per minute happening somewhere in the world.[1] There are other types of anomalies that are more localized than lightning, like the will-o-wisp lights that can be seen floating through swamps. Gasses emitted from the swamp combine to form a wispy light that has often been mistaken for someone's ghost.

Faultlines are also known culprits when it comes to emitting light energy. More often than not, the phenomena at active faultlines like the San Andreas and Blue Cut faults in California are visible. Sparks have recently been seen popping around these faultlines like ladyfinger firecrackers. It is as if Gaia is snapping her fingers to get the West Coast's attention.

Photo by Robert Firth

Lightning is just one of the ways that Gaia distributes electrical energy. Worldwide, there are approximately 6,000 strikes of lightning per minute. In recent years this number has grown, due to global weather changes.

This is not the first time Gaia has used her charms to warn of disaster. The glowing lights of St. Elmo's fire warned seamen of stormy weather,[2] and the anomalies found around the magnetic fields of Puget Sound have acted as guideposts for captains to adjust their compasses or drift off course. As we learn to read natural phenomena we expand our ability to predict its purpose. Science knows more about what makes the phenomena happen, i.e. what photon is connected to what proton, but we do not have a very good grasp on the biological effects these phenomena have on people.

Anywhere there is natural phenomena, there is energy to be explored. Remember how Ben Franklin proved this? Try not to repeat his mistake. Use the energy without connecting yourself to it, please! There is a whole world of exploration to be done in the presence of natural phenomena and there is no better time to start than now. Have fun.

AMPLIFICATION

CHAPTER 6

GALLERIES OF SONG

W̱e know that the architects of the Great Pyramid of Giza had knowledge of the energy centers in their region. They knew where the grid networks interacted, and where the ley paths began and where they ended. Energy wellsprings were accurately pinpointed, as were the magnetic anomalies of the desert. The Egyptian priests combined this knowledge with geometrical equations, then built energy-enhanced structures over the anomalies. The grandest in design is found at Giza.

The Great Pyramid is not the only example of ancient people's ability to manipulate and amplify energy frequencies. There are sacred shrines and temples all over the planet built in accordance with some higher law than the local building code. The pyramids of the Aztecs were built according to sacred prescription, as are the Mayan temples found around the Yucatan and Guatemala. The Hawaiians took special care when building their sacred temples, following the architect/priest's instructions to the letter or dying for their errors. In England, we know that Rollright and Stonehenge were systematically built to conduct or, under certain circumstances, repel specific energy frequencies.[1] This also appears to be the case with the great cathedrals of Europe, built by the mystical order of Freemasons. Research shows that the Sun Temple at Mesa Verde National Park in Colorado was built in accordance with specific Hopi architectural designs, representing through symbolic design the Bow clan and the Two and One Horn societies.[2]

These examples show us that sacred site architecture is nothing new. Structures large and small have been built all over the planet to amplify energy or mark the location of a particular anomaly. There are structures that symbolically represent the religious concepts, holy history, and the magic of certain cultures. Others represent time and place, like the solar sites and lunar sites that mark where heaven and earth meet in Chaco Canyon, New Mexico, or the Big Horn Medicine Wheel in Wyoming. If the Earth was not so cluttered we would easily recognize these places of power, but we must rely on other methods of locating them because sometimes they have been knocked down and covered up by freeways, parking lots, or mountain resorts. Fortunately, many sites have been preserved within our parks system. Others outside the system must be watched carefully, or they will soon disappear.

What I am trying to establish is that there are structures, built with varying degrees of skill, scattered throughout the Earth like galleries marking the existence of sacred sites. These structures vary in purpose. The small adobe chapel found at Chimayo, the "Lourdes of America,"

Photo by Cheyenne Rousse

Chaco Canyon, where heaven and earth meet. The Chaco community numbered in the thousands. As the Anasazi's cultural center, Chaco influenced the politics and finances of a region hundreds of miles in diameter.

is not ornate, but despite its simplicity continues to have an enormous influence on thousands of people's lives annually. It was not built to enhance energy but as a shrine or landmark, acknowledging where miracles occurred.

On the other hand, there are sites whose architecture is grandiose and elaborate—usually to amplify the local energies like those found at Delphi, the Taj Mahal, and Giza. The cathedrals of Europe are prime examples of how manipulated energy can be amplified through architecture. The Freemasons were wizards of Pythagorean geometry. They built the cathedrals according to sacred mathematical equations that had been handed down through the secret society for ages. The ultimate purpose of the amplification of energies was to achieve an optimal environment conducive to spirituality—the joining of the energies of Heaven and Earth, so to speak.

Some of the cathedrals were built on grid intersections that coincided with ley line paths. The main sanctuary's altar was placed under the highest point of the steeple; both were purposely built directly over a corresponding intersection point.[3] No doubt some powerful sermons were delivered from this location, but it was how the congregation received the message that was the real intent behind the architecture of the cathedral.

The cathedrals were said to vibrate to a specific musical note. Each cathedral had its own tone or vibration. This has been proven by experiments conducted within the sanctuaries by various artists and researchers during meditative states. Experiments have shown when groups of people meditate on the vibration within certain cathedrals they usually come up with the same note, and that note changes from cathedral to cathedral. We now know that certain musical notes affect particular parts of our mind and body. Joseph Campbell demonstrates these correlations in his book *The Mythic Image,* which is based on ancient Sanskrit formulas.[4] If, for instance, a cathedral's individual note vibrates to the key of F, matters of the heart (literally), virtue, and compassion will probably be the main focus of the church. Each note corresponds to a chakra opening, certain symbols, a body organ, and individual states of consciousness. It was the architect's goal to amplify the spirit of place of the cathedral enough to cause the pilgrim to experience an altered state resulting in a specific transformation triggered by an Earth song.

The idea that sacred site energies relate to the musical scale is found in ancient records all over our planet. Our ancestors understood

Photo by Jeff Johnson

The cathedral at Cologne, Germany, believed to be built on ley lines.

the dynamics of these relationships. They knew what site vibrated to what note and what could be healed by that note. They understood that if they dreamed about owls or eagles the site probably vibrated to the key of A. The functions of what we now call the pituitary system are stimulated by the key of A, so healings of this system would be sought out at a site that vibrated to this note. To turbo-boost beneficial frequencies through architecture results in amplified energies that not only stimulate subconscious spirituality, but physical healing as well.

The aborigines of the Australian outback describe their walk-about path as a "Line of Songs." The aborigines understood where the sacred sites were that sang the Earth song. They sometimes marked these sites with a rock cairn. A well-worn path following the "Line of Songs" was imprinted so deeply into the ground one could hardly lose the way. The world-famous Ayers Rock is one of the points of power along the Line of Songs. It upsets the natives of this area that so many people are found on and around this most holy of their sites, (noting that they are not found crawling up the sides of our sanctuaries, so please get off theirs!).[5] The striking similarity between the Freemason's musical cathedrals and the

Photo by Bernyce Barlow

The Matterhorn is an example of a point of power that, according to Carl Jung, would resonate to the key of B.

Aborigines' Line of Songs is not a coincidence. The Earth vibrates music. How a culture decides to build up or amplify the harmony of the land is individual and varies from culture to culture. What is and has always been universal is the song itself.

Carlos Nakai, the enchanting Navajo-Ute whose haunting music has brought worldwide acclaim, recorded the remarkable melodies of "Sundance Season" and "Desert Dance" during improvisational recording sessions at the Lindisfarne chapel in the San Luis Valley of Colorado. The valley itself is sacred song, a place where the Earth resonates a symphony of harmonious chords. The valley is so precious that it is protected by the Continental Divide, the Saguache Mountains, the Sangre de Christo range, and the San Juan mountains.[6] It is a place of power that Mother Nature wants safely tucked away so her song is not disrupted. Lindisfarne chapel is a modern-day sacred site, providing a holy structure where the music of the land can be translated into music for the soul. If you have any doubt, just listen to what Nakai calls his ritual about the San Luis Valley, "Desert Dance." It is the song of Gaia.

When you take your journeys to explore the sacred sites, keep in mind Gaia's song. It can be heard if you listen quietly. If you are lucky enough to find a structure that amplifies that song, you may hear it as more of an echo than a note. However the Earth song comes through to you, allow its harmony to align itself with your subconscious because that is where the meaning of the music lies. Let the song fill the vast spaces between the atoms and protons and all the other peppy particles you are made up of, so it vibrates to the very core of your being. Listen carefully to the crashing waves of the ocean and to the wind tunes in the forests. Listen to the caves that whistle and the river's rhythm and you will hear the song of Gaia in each one of them. Capture the song and you will become a living gallery, the ultimate sacred temple where the song of Gaia is enhanced through the ultimate architecture of the body, mind, and soul.

MIND AND SITE

CHAPTER 7

PERSONALIZING THE SACRED SITES

Each year, millions of people make personal pilgrimages to sacred centers of our planet such as Lourdes of France, Jerusalem, Mecca, Australia's Ayers Rock, and Chimayo, New Mexico. Worldwide, all cultures have recognized the power of certain sites and have set them aside as sacred. Most of these centers are acknowledged in one form or another from the grandiose to the simple, from majestic sacred sites such as the Pyramid of Giza and the Temple of Delphi, to places like the dreaming circles of Death Valley, California, identified only by a five-foot circle of impacted gravel polished by the harsh desert elements. These sites were not chosen at random but for their specific anomaly abilities. In the Gaia section, we examined what some of these anomalies are and how they affect us. Now let's take a closer look at mind and site.

As discussed, biochemical changes occur at the sacred centers of Gaia. Neurotransmitters like serotonin become deregulated sending and perceiving messages differently than what is considered the norm. Under the influence of the sites, our perspectives change and consciousness is heightened. Biorhythms fall into cadence with circadian rhythms, and dimensions we are not accustomed to are brought into the light.

37

Photo by Deb Olson

Prayer stones indicate this site had spiritual significance to someone.

The end result of all this intellectual deregulation often induces something called by Carl Jung an ecstacy state. There are three kinds of ecstacy states: ademic, union, and knowledge.[1] Energy anomalies found at sacred sites trigger these states, as well as amplify their internal purpose.

Although there are three different kinds of ecstacy states, only one formula governs their overall behavior. The average ecstacy state experience lasts thirty to forty minutes. It has a trigger point, a realization point, a peak, a power point, and, last, an inspired integration of knowledge to be utilized personally.

Ademic states are usually experienced by folks who have come to the end of their rope. The emotions felt by people preceding an ademic state are usually depression, fear, hopelessness, or abandonment. Suddenly, a light bulb turns on—an idea, a life change, an understanding, an acceptance of whatever it will take to change the mood enough to change the circumstance.

We have all seen movies where the heartbroken lover walks along the beach alone, absorbed in grief and loss, when suddenly an attitude of acceptance and confidence emerges from something realized during her stroll. The next thing you see is the actress dancing along the shoreline, kicking water up with her toes, heading into the sunset smiling and contented. Some call this a happy ending. I call it an ademic ecstacy experience!

A union ecstacy state is quite different than an ademic state. Union states usually happen in places of harmony and unquestionable beauty, and leave such an overwhelming imprint that the experience stays with the person for a lifetime. Universal truths are brought up from the subconscious to the conscious during a union ecstacy state, and feelings of awe and divine respect are often associated with the experience.[2]

I believe most people who can get out of the city can encounter a union ecstacy state. I have heard of folks, especially well-trained athletes, who achieve a type of union state when pushing their bodies to the limit (not to be confused with a runner's high).[3] Since most of us are not marathon runners or world class athletes, we can use the inspiration and energies of Gaia to trigger union consciousness.

Photo by Doug Deutscher

Canyons of the Colorado River trigger multiple ecstasy experiences. Farther downriver in the Grand Canyon, Havasupai Falls is an excellent site in which to explore ecstacy states.

If someone really wants to experience a union state, I tell them to float the Colorado River in the canyonlands of Utah or Arizona. Along the Colorado, places of power are marked by rock art and small ruins that stand sentry over the river. There are other sites that are not marked at all; you have to see them with an inner eye, but the energy of these places, when combined with the inspiring beauty of the region, always triggers some kind of a state whether you are looking for it or not. Because of the extraordinary beauty and physics of the canyonlands, union states are experienced more often than ademic or knowledge states, although union ecstacy can lead into a knowledge state quite smoothly, a double whammy!

A knowledge ecstacy state is less personal, giving individuals insight into the values of intellectual and academic nature—the "now I get it" experience. Einstein was a knowledge ecstacy freak as most progressive thinkers are. It appears the more one pushes his/her potential, the more potential is pushed through that person. Gifts of academic revelation often come in the form of knowledge ecstacy, which can get somewhat addictive, especially if you are into subjects like the Theory of Relativity.

After examining the states of ecstacy that are triggered by the spirit of place, it is no wonder that pilgrimages have been made to these sites since early times. Ecstacy states reflect healing and truth, two levels of behavior borrowed from the I AM consciousness. Therefore, it is not at all unusual for people to seek out these levels at their seat of power.

Because of the unique spirit of place each sacred site possesses, individual experiences will vary, but the collective experience of the site will display a familiar flavor. Understanding the intelligent purpose of a place of power will also allow you to channel your energies in the right direction.

There are sacred sites everywhere. If you do not know of any in your area, ask around. Power spots are usually hard to keep secret, but bear in mind they are special, and treat them as such.

It is important that we be aware of the mystique of sacred sites, not only for their personal application but for their protection. Many places of power now have parking lots, fantasy accommodations, and malls built on top of them. To destroy these sites is to destroy part of the precious heritage passed on to us from Gaia. If we accept the fact the Earth was created from some kind of divine inspiration we will be better served, especially when standing on holy ground.

CHAPTER 8

THE SCHUMANN RESONANCE

In therapeutic circles you hear a lot about what is called the Schumann Resonance. It is created by a pattern of brain waves that have fallen into a particular rhythm or cadence. What makes the brain waves act in this fashion is internal or external influence. A Schumann Resonance can be reached through various meditation techniques by slowing down the body's systems enough to achieve a hertz rate that falls between three and fourteen. The resonance can also be triggered by the spirit of place at a sacred site.

Hertz means "second." If the brain waves fall into a cycle between three and fourteen hertz, specific conditions develop. People become more creative, health conditions are more likely to be maintained or healed, visualization is enhanced, and an overall feeling of well being is imparted to the individual experiencing the resonance. Ecstacy states often occur while under this influence and people who have the ability to heal do so around eight hertz, as do those who receive the healing. Ten hertz is a good frequency for enhanced visualization and circadian control.[1]

The Schumann Resonance also seems to aid in healing emotional wounds that are carried deep within the spirit. When working with a wounded soul, healing cannot take place until you get beyond the hurt to somewhere the abuse didn't touch. That place becomes the cornerstone for renewal and it can be reached through the Schumann Resonance. In therapy, I have used the resonance often. There are many ways to achieve this state. It was not often practical to pack up a bunch of rowdy kids to visit a resonance site, so I used other techniques instead. Music, aromatherapy, and guided visualization all together in one package usually worked. The kids called it "woo-woo therapy" and used the time to explore the parts of their minds that were safe. After learning the technique, the groups looked forward to site therapy, knowing they could achieve the same safe state of mind without all the work.

Photo by Bernyce Barlow

The Schumann Resonance is evident in the Boynton Canyon area near Sedona. The elements have carved the coconino sandstone into fairy-like castle formations, citadels and towers, a wonderful playland to romp through. Many Anasazi ruins are found in Boynton Canyon.

The hertz rate at sacred sites more often than not falls into the Schumann Resonance. Folklorist and counselor Oz Johnson talks about the effect the resonance had on her while visiting Oak Creek Canyon near Flagstaff, Arizona.

"The top of my head started to tingle, as if the higher chakras were opening up. It was not an effect I was trying to achieve; it just happened. Later, after I had settled into the site a flood of memories concerning my late father seemed to work their way down from the top chakra through the first. I felt as if he was aware of me and sent a small cloud, like a sky dot, as a reminder that he was around. The experience left me with the feeling I was dearly loved. When I went to the site I had no intention of dealing with memories of my father, but the spirit of place gently passed the message on anyway."

Ms. Johnson's experience is a good example of how the Schumann Resonance acts as a neurological buffer. It allows sensitive information to be processed without a reaction. As the kids would say, "it takes the edge off." Sites that trigger the Schumann Resonance also enhance creativity. When the edge is gone, creative juices are allowed to flow, sparking consciousness into an artistic wildfire.

Photo by Deb Olson

This active fissure in Volcano National Park has a high hertz rate. Human resonance can still be achieved there through meditation.

The geophysical frequencies that create the Schumann resonance can also cause havoc with our biological functions. Places that are located on spots that generate higher hertz rates—like active faultlines, fissures, volcanos, and locations with negative (polarity, not vibes) magnetic energy—tend to make people ill. Reports of headaches, anxiety, and loss of sleep are the norm in these areas. Just ask anyone living close to the San Andreas faultline in Southern California, or near Washington's Mount St. Helens just before she blew up. Fortunately, most of the earth's surface does not generate these types of frequencies, but it helps to be aware of them because they do occur occasionally.

Fortunately, there are places that we can retreat to that aid our well being. The Schumann Resonance seems to influence our mind and body to accept healing, spiritual identification, and creative enrichment. When other earth energies like negative ions or ley intersections are combined with the resonance, all kinds of possibilities open up, depending on what anomalies are available at any given site. The Schumann Resonance is one of the keys that opens the door to a sacred center, allowing the spirit of place to peek through. What a delightful way to begin a journey that may whisk you away on a magic carpet spun from the dreams and earthsongs of Gaia.

CHAPTER 9

CHIMAYO: THE LOURDES OF AMERICA

N estled in the foothills of New Mexico's Sangre de Cristo mountain
range is a little town of miracles called Chimayo. Chimayo's history is fairly well documented, going back to the late 1500s. It was
settled in 1598 as the easternmost outpost for the Province of New
Mexico. The town survived the pueblo uprisings but it was not until
1696 that Chimayo settled down enough to become a legend.

The Lourdes of America is what Chimayo is called today. During
holy week thousands of pilgrims travel from all over the world, seeking
a miracle at the chapel called the Santuario De Nuestro Senor De Equipulas. They come to pray, praise, and partake of the sacred dirt that can
be found in a small annex called the *El Posito* (little well room), next to
the chapel. The Catholic church has chosen not to investigate reports of
miraculous healings at Chimayo but readily acknowledges they appear
to happen there, giving credit to the healing spirit of Christ.[1]

As is the case with many sacred sites, the Santuario has a colorful
history that helps us track the origin of the chapel's reputation. In order
to do that, we must go back to the era when the Spanish arrived in the
Mayan jungles of what is now Guatemala. A wise Mayan leader, Equipulas, was able to negotiate a peaceful settlement between his people
and the Spaniards.

When the Spaniards sought to introduce the Christian religion to the Mayans, Equipulas advised that the image of Christ be dark-skinned like his people. The Mayans had seen many atrocities at the hands of the Spaniards and would not likely worship a fair-skinned god. The great Portuguese woodcarver, Quiro Catano, was commissioned to create a

Photo by Bernyce Barlow

The adobe Chapel at Chimayo, the "Lourdes of America," is considered a place of miracles. Thousands of pilgrims come to this chapel each year for healing and celebration.

five-foot sculptured crucifix out of balsam and orange wood for the town and people of Equipulas. The carving was called the Black Christ, and hung on a dark green cross embossed with gold vines.[2]

The cross was said to be the focal point for a number of healings that happened in Central America. In 1737, the archbishop of Guatemala said he was healed of a contagious disease at Equipulas. From that point on the shrine became renowned for its healing miracles.

It is important to note that the shrine had been built near a network of mineral springs and mud pools that had been frequented by the Mayans for hundreds of years before the Spanish arrived. Ingestion of the local clay was said to have beneficial results for some afflictions and was used in a variety of homeopathic remedies by the Indians. It is not surprising that one of the rituals that developed around the prescribed ceremony at Equipulas included the ingestion of holy dirt.

So what does this all have to do with Chimayo? Sometime before 1805, Bernardo Abeyta brought the cult of Equipulas from Guatemala to New Mexico. How Senor Abeyta knew of the practices at the Shrine of Equipulas is not known. It is known, however, that he introduced a replica of the Black Christ into a chapel that he built in the Potrero district near Chimayo around 1816. He dedicated the chapel in the name of Our Lord of Equipulas.

How the Black Christ replica arrived in Chimayo contributes to the folklore accompanying documented history of the area. One legend says that Abeyta, after seeing a light shining from the ground, felt compelled to dig up the spot, and found a crucifix. Abeyta and the townspeople carried the cross to Santa Cruz to be displayed, but the cross disappeared from the chapel in Santa Cruz only to magically reappear in Chimayo. This was said to have happened three times. Finally, the community left the cross at its point of origin, somewhat awed by its mystique. The Santuario was built by Abeyta, on the spot where he said he found the six-foot green cross.[3]

At this point, a new cult of Equipulas was established, including the concept of consuming or using the clay or dirt for healing. Today, this practice has integrated itself into the rituals performed by many of the pilgrims who visit the Santuario de Chimayo, especially during Holy Week. The crucifix can be seen in the Santuario behind the altar but is often overshadowed by the reputation of El Posito.

As far back as the 1850s, settlement disputes and what appears to be revenue jealousy not only changed the nature of the Santuario but its saints. Today, the Sons of the Holy Family Order preserves the history, changes, and clarity of Chimayo through education and an openness to the biblical phrase, "all things are possible through Christ."

Because we do not know the origin of the Black Christ of Chimayo, history has left mystery to fill in the blanks. For some this mystery is the catalyst for the faith it takes to experience miracles. For others, faith is the force that helps create the spirit of place at the shrine. Spiritual commitment is a tremendous energy force that can and has altered lives physically and emotionally on a grandiose scale. When thousands and thousands gather together in faith, this energy force has the ability to affect the most casual visitor, for at this point faith becomes physics.

Regardless of whether we look at the history, the faith, or the physics of Chimayo, it is important to note that the site holds a certain sacredness. If a person had the qualities of Chimayo, that person would be considered holy. Many who visit Chimayo have no idea of its history, nor do they care. They only know of its reputation as a shrine of miracles and of the personal faith that brought them there.

There is an undeniable peace surrounding Chimayo. You can find it beneath the cottonwood trees that grow on the banks of the nearby Santa Cruz river in the summer, or along the snow-lined dirt roads of the foothills above the Santuario in early spring. The streets, the courtyards, and the plaza all have a feel of security and serenity. Mystique has not gone under holy ground at Chimayo—indeed it remains a place where people can go to demonstrate the power in which they believe. For this reason alone, the blessed earth of Chimayo will always be considered sacred ground.

Photo by Berryce Barlow

Mass at Chimayo is held outside, weather permitting. The peace and serenity of Chimayo reward all who make the pilgrimage to this holy site.

CHAPTER 10

PU'UHONUA O HONAUNAU

On the Kona Coast, along the shores of Honauna Bay, is an area of enchantment called Pu'uhonua O Honaunau, or the City of Refuge. The spirit of place at this tropical wonderland is vibrant and strong. This is due in part to the carefully preserved holy history of the refuge, but the powerful and unique energy fields found around Honauna Bay signal the human neurological system to jump start, adding to the ambiance of the site.

Pu'uhonua O Honaunau cradles a very sacred spirit of place, one of sanctuary and life. Old Hawaiian culture was governed by certain laws or *kapus*. If a kapu was broken the penalty was death, because islanders believed that to break a kapu was to offend the gods. When the gods got angry they retaliated in all sorts of ways: lava flows, disease, infertility, and hurricanes. It was, therefore, a priority to keep the gods happy.

The kapu system governed everything. Each hour of the day had its own set of kapus. The ruling classes used the kapus to their advantage, keeping the best privileges reserved for themselves. To look at a chief or walk where his shadow had once fallen could result in death. To fish or eat at the wrong time, or eat in mixed company, also could result in death. When a kapu was broken, the offender was hunted

Photo by Deb Olson

Hale o Keawe, the heiau at the City of Refuge, was the final resting place of at least twenty-three island chiefs. The last one was said to be the grandson of Kamehameha II.

like an animal until caught and put to death, unless he could make it to the gates of the City of Refuge where he would be given absolution.[1]

If the Pu'uhonua was reached, the *kahuna pule*, or priest, would conduct a ceremony that granted absolution to the offender and he could go home, usually within a few hours. During the fifteenth and sixteenth centuries, there were two refuges on the island of Hawaii: Honaunau in the south, and one adjunct to the heiau of Paakalani on the northern coast. These two refuges were the only locations where absolutions were performed.[2]

Absolution was not the only function of the refuge. It was also a place of protection from the violent and exacting district wars. Since the object of battle was complete annihilation of the opponent, noncombatants such as the very young or the very old were given sanctuary within the refuge. Defeated warriors also waited out the battles on refuge grounds in turn for their allegiance when the next battle rolled around. Honaunau saw lots of action during the 1550s–1700s, due to many island disputes.

The Great Wall that surrounds the City of Refuge was probably built around 1500, to honor Keawe-ku-i-ke-ka'ai, the ruling chief of the era. It was built in an L-shape, separating the palace grounds from the refuge itself. It measures approximately 1,000 feet long, ten feet high, and seventeen feet wide. The wall was a powerful symbol to the islanders as to the strength of their character, but it could not compete with the power of the heiau within it.

Hawaiians believed the ruling chiefs had a special mana or power given to them by the gods. Even after death the mana remained in their bones. Heiaus or temples were built to house the bones in order

Photo by Bernyce Barlow

Hawaiian Tiki inside the walls at Hale o Keawe helps to guard the royal remains. Stolen bones were carved into rodent spearheads and fishhooks to debase and humiliate the deceased king's family.

to collect the mana. The more bones there were in the temple, the more power there was at the heiau. By 1818, the bones of at least twenty-three island chiefs had been laid to rest at Hale O Keawe, the heiau now standing at the City of Refuge.

Two other heiaus existed at the refuge before Hale O Keawe was built. A-le'ale'a was built before 1550, and a heiau now being studied appears to be older than A-le'ale'a. It was not uncommon during a war to try and steal the mana from a heiau. That is why some of the greatest rulers of Hawaii had their bones hidden in jungle caves so their power could never be misused.

Most visitors report that by the time they learn the holy history of the City of Refuge the physics of the site has also been absorbed. The most obvious law of physics at work here is the generation of negative ions. Several forces of nature are constantly in motion at Honaunau. The rhythm of the waves crashing down on the hardened lava shores and the lapping of the sea at Keone'ele cove continuously bathe the refuge in negative ions. More are created as the Trade Winds sway *niu* (coconut) trees gently, like palace fans. The abundant negative ion count complements the other energies at the site.

There is some question whether Pu'uhonau Honaunau is a positive electromagnetic vortex or not. It certainly feels like one, but the energies there do not conform to the usual vortex patterns. Nevertheless, life takes on a surrealistic edge within the influence of this site. Time slows down, colors are vibrant, sounds and scents are clean, and the imagination is sparked by the energy of the land.

It is easy to fall into the Schumann Resonance at the refuge, resulting in a calm, serene state where creativity and spirituality are enhanced. There is a very relaxed feeling around Honaunau, and after a while you will slow down too. Visualization abilities are particularly heightened at the refuge, as is automatic writing.

The kahuna pules were attracted to Pu'uhonua because of its mystery and power. They chose sites like Honaunau because the local energies of the land complemented the mana of the gods within their heiaus. There is much mystery hidden beneath the volcanic sands of Honaunau that may never be completely uncovered. The nui trees know the answers, but never whisper loud enough to be heard by mortals, so we must look to ourselves for revelation. It may be reflected in the royal fish ponds that belonged to the chiefs, or etched into the bark of the nui tree, but the answers are there. It is just a matter of looking in the right place at the City of Refuge.

CHAPTER 11

CATARACT CANYON

S hades of gold, amber, rust, and orange set one on top of another, interwoven by time, cast a glow in Cataract Canyon that the finest artist could not re-create. You have only to look at the layers of stratum, 2 billion to 250 million years old, displayed upon the face of the canyon walls, to truly appreciate the infancy of the human race upon this planet. Within Cataract Canyon one cannot help but feel it is here among the colors of the sun that the history of the West began.

The first official mapping and exploration of the Colorado river, including Cataract Canyon, was completed by the John Wesley Powell expedition. In May of 1869, Powell and nine men set out to challenge the Colorado river. Four months later their task was complete, but not without loss. Three members of the expedition had been killed. At one time it was assumed the members of the crew had been killed by the native residents of the region. Today, there are theories circulating that point to Mormon interference with the expedition's goals. The debate continues.

Cataract Canyon is directly above Lake Powell, Utah. The canyon has the steepest incline of any on the Colorado River, and officially begins where the equally impressive Green River and the Colorado converge. The canyon has twenty-eight sets of rapids, some with class

5 ratings. High water can reach 65,000 cubic feet per second, making Cataract Canyon unequaled in North America for triggering a white-water adrenaline rush.[1]

With names like the Big Drops 1, 2, and 3, Ben Hurt, Imperial, and Number 10, these rapids tumble downhill, exhibiting tremendous power. They are considered as dangerous in low water as in high water. J-rig and S-rig World War II pontoon rafts negotiate the river with as much care as did the wooden boats of Powell's expedition. The rapids are a thrilling part of the exploration of this region, and are a necessary part of the trip if you are to enjoy the hidden treasures found within the 120-mile stretch between Moab and Lake Powell, Utah.

Once you get accustomed to the ride down the river, your attention may turn to the side canyons that are full of historical and spiritual sites. Indian Creek Canyon is a sixteen-mile-long side canyon that connects to the San Juan Basin. It was used 2,000 years ago by the Anasazi as a corridor between the basin and the river. Hundreds of artifacts,

Photo by Bernyce Barlow

The Big Drops Rapids in Cataract Canyon holds the author's J-rig raft hostage. This thrilling, white-water route is not for the faint-hearted.

ruins, wall peckings, cliff paintings, and granaries can be found throughout Indian Creek Canyon.[2]

Fossil Canyon is a few miles below the Indian Creek area. Huge boulders there are covered with selenite crystals that sparkle when the sun hits them just right. This effect gives the canyon an enchantment that is difficult to describe. Fossil Canyon has earned its name—there are fossils everywhere. Most prevalent are the ocean fossils, but dinosaur bones are also found in this canyon.

Photo by Bernyce Barlow

Ocean fossil found in Fossil Canyon, Utah.

There are other side canyons along the river where Anasazi ruins stand sentry, and whose only visitors are the Bighorn sheep seeking shade from the harsh sun. You see these ruins and wonder if others before you felt the same kind of awe and curiosity you are feeling as the sun casts shadows on precariously perched granaries. Little has changed here—little *can* change here. It is a place of time-transcending beauty whose history and treasures have been kept safe by intimidating gates of whitewater and mile-high sheer cliffs. There is something comforting about knowing much of the West's most precious history is safe within these boundaries and will continue to be safe from disturbance for some time.

The physics of the Cataract region induce ecstacy states. A myriad of individual and combined energy forces are found throughout the canyon. An added benefit to the spirit of place of the Cataract is the high concentration of uranium found in the soil. It was only a few decades ago that the fashionable thing to do was drink uranium water for healing. It was a fad that did not stop until people started drop-

Photo by Bernyce Barlow

Anasazi Ruin in Indian Creek Canyon, a side canyon of Cataract Canyon in Utah. This ruin's inhabitants farmed and hunted along the Colorado River around A.D. 1000.

ping dead. Uranium is a powerful generator of negative ions; its use is carefully controlled.

Cataract Canyon is not the most sacred center. The ride down the river is not for everyone, but if you do not mind sand, suds, and an occasional adrenaline rush, this trip is well worth the grit. There is plenty of time to reflect as you free-float down the Colorado, past rock cathedrals and fairy castle formations. You can watch eagles ride the wind and lose yourself in the sky, and at night when the stars come out you again find yourself a part of the heavens. Cataract Canyon will both ground you and send you soaring—a fine combination of energy that makes for a great journey.

CHAPTER 12

SANTA CATALINA ISLAND

The island of Santa Catalina is one of eight isles of enchantment that lie just off the coast of southern California. Collectively, these islands are called the Santa Barbara Channel Islands. At its closest point, Catalina island is only nineteen miles from the mainland, but when you arrive there you feel as if the two are a world apart, and in a way they are. Most of the mainland sits on the North American plate, but Catalina rests on the tectonic Pacific plate. Unlike some of the other islands in the Channel chain, twenty-one-mile-long Catalina was formed by volcanic activity and plate movement. The Chumash tribe called Catalina "mountain ranges that rise from the sea."[1]

Catalina's history is colorful and lively. There is an ambiance of mystery that can be felt all over the island. Over the last 30,000 years a handful of prehistoric cultures lived among the Channel Islands. They left a kind of historical mystique behind that can be clearly felt along the island chain. Archaeologists have found artifacts dating as far back as 19,000 years, but the main body of tangible finds are dated between 2000 B.C. through the late 1700s. There are hundreds of middens scattered throughout the islands that have given researchers mounds of information to dig through. There are hundreds more not yet excavated that will add to the data already collected.

Returning the focus to Santa Catalina, it is easy to see why the largest aboriginal populations inhabited this island. It was not only a beautiful paradise but the island provided an abundance of game and sea supplies for survival and trade. There appear to be three main areas that hosted communities: Little Harbor, Two Harbors, and Avalon. Two Harbors was the largest community and Little Harbor is considered the

Photo by Bernyce Barlow

Sculpture called "The First Islander," a tribute to Catalina's native population, is found on the Avalon side of the island, on the way to Wrigley Gardens.

oldest. Because these three areas are located close to the sea, with a supply of fresh water, they were the obvious choices for settlement.

The islanders called themselves Pimugnans and their island Pimu. The Pimugnan's linguistic link to the Shoshonean civilization gives us a hint as to the ancestry of the most recent aboriginal tribe of Catalina, but active interaction with the mainland Chumash impacted the culture tremendously. The Pimugnans eventually adopted many of the Chumash customs and integrated them into their religious and social beliefs.

Exceptional evidence left behind by the Pimugnans has allowed us to put together a fairly accurate view of their lifestyle. There are also the accounts of the Spaniards, beginning around 1542, who renamed the islanders Gabrielenos. These writings afford us a more modern perspective of the early inhabitants of the island whereas the middens give us a more ancient view. What we do know about the Pimugnans is that they enjoyed a rich lifestyle dependent on the land, sea, and fresh water. The Pimu band was said to emulate the Chumash culture in its purest form.

The most ancient site, at Little Harbor, is a good place to begin to study the holy history of Pimu. Tucked into the hills in the Little Harbor area are places to explore that showcase the sacred ways. There are obsidian quarries, caves with rock art, middens, grinding and tool grounds, and sacred springs throughout the area. With a little time and effort you may be rewarded with the discovery of one of these ancient sites.

The obsidian on Catalina was considered powerful magic by many of the tribes of the west and southwest. Carvings or talismans were made from the revered Pimu obsidian, then traded on the mainland. Archaeologists have found Pimu obsidian carvings in villages as far away as New Mexico, substantiating the belief that the Pimugnan were mystical as well as aggressive traders. Ceremonies and rituals that took place in the Little Harbor community have left a strong imprint for the visitor to sense. Along with ceremonies involving the sacred obsidian were rites that belonged to the Chingichnich cult, a religion presided over by a hierarchy of shamans and political chiefs that was popular among the southern coastal California tribes. Many of the painted caves found on the island are directly connected to ceremonies performed by shamans under the influence of hallucinogenic drugs.

The mainland population considered the islanders magicians— wizards who had power over the elements. Legends about a great temple called a *yuva'r* describe a sacred complex of worship where all

Photo by Bernyce Barlow

View from Mount Ada, Catalina Island, looking down to Avalon Bay. All along the coast are caves once used by the early tribes.

the natives of the Channel Islands came to celebrate once a year. The Vizcaino expedition of 1602 recorded the existence of such a yuva'r in the Two Harbors area. The yuva'r was described as an open-air temple held together with poles and banners decorated with vibrant feathers. It was off limits to all but the elder tribal holy men of power. The ruins of one of these great temples is still sought in the Two Harbors area by both professional and amateur archaeologists. The remains of other yuva'rs have been found on the island, adding to the mystique of this enchanted isle.[2]

Since the waters around Catalina were teeming with seal, otter, and other fur-bearing mammals, the Pimugnans were involved in a flourishing fur commerce. They were primarily hunters and traders. Later, the opulent waters of Catalina attracted greedy foreigners who wanted to harvest all the fur. This abundance of game eventually led to the demise of the islanders, for the outsiders who eventually came to Pimu wanted the Pimugnan gone, and by 1832 they were history.

In 1806 a large company was formed between the Russian-American Fur Company in Sitka, Alaska, and two American entrepreneurs. With boats full of aggressive Aleut and Kodiak Indians from Alaska, the company set sail to ravage the waters surrounding the Channel Islands.

The members of the northern tribes refused to co-exist with the Pimug-nans. They looted villages, raped Pimugnan women, captured their children, and slaughtered the Pimu men. The remaining Pimu popula-tion was mowed down by the diseases that came on the trader ships. Some of the Pimugnan found their way to the mainland and were assimilated into the mission system. All in all, it was a very sad ending for this peaceful, friendly people.

With the Pimugnans gone, pirates, smugglers, and traders used the pristine coves of Catalina for everything from hiding Chinese immigrants to concealing pirate contraband. There was even a gold rush of sorts in the 1860s. During this period of exploitation the sea mammal population was totally decimated throughout the Channel Islands.Wild pigs and goats were also introduced to Catalina and plundered the natural vegetation of the island to near extinction. The influences brought to Catalina from the outside nearly changed the island's personality permanently.

Private ownership of Catalina began in 1846 (at the close of the Mexican War) when the Mexican governor, Pio Pico, signed the title over to the American Thomas Robbins. Perhaps the most well-known owner of Catalina was the chewing gum king, William Wrigley Jr. who passed on the controlling stock of the island to his son, Philip. Philip Wrigley created a non-profit conservancy that to this day preserves and protects Catalina. Little by little, the conservancy is restoring the island's original ecosystem. Sea otter and seal are once again abundant in the coves, as are the sea birds and undersea life around the island. There may never be a complete restoration of the island but the efforts made in the name of Gaia have been valiant and important to the health and future of Catalina.[3]

This is a thumbnail historical sketch at best, but it gives you a feel for the holy history of Catalina. The incredible beauty of the island speaks for itself. At times, Catalina is undeniably romantic. At other times it seems wistful, full of play and enchantment. Catalina has many moods, sometimes changing from sunrise to sunset. It is her nature to change often. As you hike the island's interior or explore its coast, dis-covery will surround you above water and below. Catalina is a diver's paradise, due in part to its clear water and in part to the variety of col-orful marine life found off its shores.

After a trek in the outback the amenities of downtown Avalon are often welcome. There you will find shops, galleries, accommodations, fine dining, and entertainment. The main marina from which most visitors arrive and depart is also located at Avalon. The town is the jump-off point for most guests, although it is possible to arrange transportation directly to Two Harbors with some shuttles. Once in Avalon most people hike, bicycle, or shuttle into the interior of the island to explore its beauty. Some visitors never make it out of Avalon because there is so much to do there. To be fair, give yourself a weekend to explore Catalina. It is difficult to see the island in any less time, although it has been done!

The Catalina of today has contrasting charms. There are rolling hills, and pristine meadows grow to the edge of steep cliffs that dramatically drop to the sea. Buffalo and fox roam the interior, and dolphin, otter, and seal patrol the shoreline. The water found in the coves is as intensely blue as a summer morning sky and the dominant colors of the earth are green and sunshiny hues. The island wildflowers come in all colors, as do the birds and butterflies that accent the landscape. After spending some time on Catalina, the visitor welcomes the contrasts as exquisite examples of the island's charm and personality.

When you combine the ambiance of Catalina with its history and mystery you have an almost perfect sacred site exploration spot. I encourage you to visit "the mountain ranges that rise from the sea" next time you find yourself in sunny Southern California.

CHAPTER 13

OAK CREEK CANYON

O ak Creek meanders through one of the most beautiful canyons in the West. Visitors to this area are greeted first by the salmon-orange, rouge-colored cliffs that give the canyon its glow. Red is a color that triggers us neurologically; it stimulates and exhilarates! The color of the canyon gives us a hint of the strong and vibrant character of the spirit of place of Oak Creek. The area has a very noticeable circadian rhythm due to a wellspring of energy that is turned on like a faucet full blast. Under the best of circumstances the energy here is difficult to harness, but after a while you get a feel for it and begin to integrate it into your experience.

Historically, Oak Creek was recognized as a purification site by Native Americans, and it is still used in that capacity today.[1] When Native Americans talk about purification they speak in terms of balance and harmony. Purification sites have the ability to drive out disharmony and create balance. They polish up the aura, energize the body, and help heal the emotional bumps and bruises we tend to pick up here and there. It is not only the body that is cleansed at purification sites, but the mind and spirit as well.

Another ceremony that takes place at Oak Creek is one of renewal. In the red rock canyon one finds the ability to focus on priorities, not

Photo by Bernyce Barlow

Along the West Fork Trail in Oak Creek Canyon, one of the region's most powerful anomalies can be experienced, especially just before the Summer Solstice.

grocery list priorities but the ones that make life meaningful. The spirit of place of Oak Creek provides an ambiance that allows the feeling of renewal to take charge, a spirit of new beginnings, a spirit of empowerment. Many journeys have begun in Oak Creek Canyon following a purification and renewal ceremony.

Although the entire Oak Creek area is spectacular, there is one place that seems to stand out. The West Fork Trail in Oak Creek Canyon leads to a sacred site with few rivals for energy and beauty, the origin of the wellspring that provides the canyon with so much personality. Here also is the largest concentration of species of flora anywhere in Arizona.[2] This trail is a wonderful place to visit after a personal purification and renewal experience. All life comes together in harmony here and a renewed spirit fits in nicely.

Enhanced dreaming is another benefit found in Oak Creek Canyon. Visitors report vivid and colorful dreams, often having a Native American theme. Personal experience tells me this is true. Dreaming patterns in Oak Creek take on a character of their own if you can get to sleep and stay asleep. Because of the energetic frequencies of the area some people find it difficult to sleep soundly, especially near the West Fork Trail during certain parts of the year. The week before the summer solstice is a particularly active time for wellspring and dreaming encounters.

There are "places of light," and Oak Creek Canyon is one of them in the truest sense of the word. According to *Strong's Concordance*, the word "light" was used as a verb in certain circumstances. *Elauno* is a Greek verb meaning light. It describes a force that pushes like oars or the wind, "to push away from." When you turn on a light switch what happens? Darkness is pushed out. Places of light drive out darkness— be it in our bodies, our minds, or our souls. The Native Americans understood that Oak Creek was a place of light and used its energies to drive out the disharmony in their lives. The physics of Oak Creek has not changed through the years. It is still a place to come to when you feel the need to start over, or to drive out darkness. The spirit of place understands its role as the generator in this procedure and turns on the neuro switch that begins the process of healing.

Within the sanctuary of Oak Creek Canyon, Oak Creek, and the West Fork Trail are a string of sites that provide us with the opportunity to cleanse ourselves in light. Expect to feel energetic and glad to be alive while visiting this sacred site, but be careful not to overdo it. You may feel like a mountain goat who desires to bound through

Photo by Robert Firth

The waters of Oak Creek Canyon are considered to have purification and renewal properties. The Oak Creek Canyon overlook located on Highway 89A between Flagstaff and Sedona is a great place to center yourself before descending into the canyon.

the canyon at an incredible pace. This feeling can be deceiving because you are not a mountain goat and you will need to slow yourself down just a bit for safety's sake. When you visit the Oak Creek area, come with an attitude of respect and reverence, and it will be amplified. When you leave the canyon, leave knowing that you have been renewed for a reason—that the light which is found in you must be passed to others along the way, for it is a light of action with a purpose that is now a part of you. Keep it shining!

CHAPTER 14

THE INDIAN CANYONS OF PALM SPRINGS

W hen people think about Palm Springs they visualize golf courses, fountains, and tennis courts galore, and for good reason. "The Desert" is where movie stars, politicians, and multimillion-dollar snowbirds migrate for the winter. It is a place where flash and cash glisten, catching the eye of the tourist population that is drawn here for sun and fun. But the real wealth of Palm Springs is not found downtown, or in the outlying towns of Palm Desert or Rancho Mirage. It is found in the canyons that are tucked away into the mountains directly behind the city. They are called the Indian Canyons.

The ancestors of the Agua Caliente Cahuilla Indians lived in the canyonlands of Palm Springs. The canyons provided shelter from the hot desert sun and water to irrigate their crops. Vegetation was abundant in the area, providing food, medicine plants, and game to ensure their survival. Because the region supported a stable lifestyle, communities were established up and down the canyon network.

There are five canyons: Palm, Chino, Tahquitz, Murray, and Andreas. Today we see reminders of the people who once lived here in the rock art etched into the nooks and crannies of the landscape. In Andreas

Photo by Bernyce Barlow

Grinding stones found in Andreas Canyon were once used to crush palm seeds into oil and flour. Herbs such as sage and wild oat were also part of the desert culture diet.

Canyon, mortars and metates whose sides are worn and smooth are embedded in the larger river rocks near the creek. It is easy to imagine the women of the community meeting here to process food while chatting about the day's events. Dams, trails and age-old reservoirs date back to the time when the canyons were an agricultural oasis on the edge of the desert. Within the Indian Canyons lies a wealth of information and history that is accessible to the most casual of visitors.

Venturing further into the canyon network, the spirit of place seems to guide you. Red-tail hawks soar on the spice wind climbing up from the desert floor, and if you are lucky you will see wild ponies or Big Horn sheep negotiating the rocky terrain in the higher areas. Adding mystique to the scenery, coyote dart in and out of rock formations, blending in with the shadows. Among the palms you are surrounded by life, and can see the intricate interaction of the players. Because of the stark contrast between the lush canyons and the barren desert floor, life has literally taken root in the Indian Canyons. Palm and Andreas Canyons boast the first and second most palm trees in the world with Murray Canyon coming in fourth. In Andreas canyon alone, over 150 species of plants have been identified.[14] This cornucopia of life is what the Indian Canyons are all about, and given half a chance, this is what the spirit of place shows visitors.

Hummingbirds proliferate throughout the canyons. At the trading post at Palm Canyon these tiny gems converge on the place, especially from November through May. Feeders have been set up to attract the birds and their numbers are incredible. Folks come from all over to see the hummingbirds of Palm Canyon. Ancient legend says the hummingbird brings good luck. If this is so, Palm Canyon is one of the luckiest places on earth.

Photo by Bernyce Barlow

When the snow fell on San Jacinto, the native population wintered over here in Andreas Canyon. Signs of their occupation can be found throughout the site.

Photo by Bernyce Barlow

Palm Canyon boasts more palm trees per square foot than any other place in the world.

The holy history of the canyons, as well as the life within them, helps us to recognize their specialness, but their unique qualities do not stop there. The San Andreas fault divides into two main branches, the Banning and Mission Creek faults, right behind Palm Springs and neighboring Cathedral City. The hills wedged between the two faultlines are called the Indio Hills, the location of the Indian Canyons. The springs mark where fault movement has broken rock deep in the earth, creating underground dams. This movement forced the electrically charged subterranean water to rise to the surface, creating the environment of the oasis canyonlands. The geophysics of this area results in a spectacular wellspring of energy.

Within the Indian Canyons there is a sacredness as life unfolds beneath the fronds of thousands of palms. Beyond is a desert scarce in landscape and unforgiving in character, a line in the sand with abundance on one side and struggle on the other. The canyons represent sanctuary not just from the fickle ways of the desert but a sanctuary from the chaos of modern living. Everything is in prescribed order in the canyons and it does not take long to fall under their spell. If you get the opportunity to visit the Indian Canyons, look for wealth that goes beyond the million-dollar swimming pools and fancy cars of the area. Look for the riches found in the windsong rustling among the palms or in the cry of the coyote. It is the kind of wealth that stays with you even if the money is gone. It is the type of wealth that belongs to the richest kind of tapestry, the tapestry of life.

CHAPTER 15

MOUNT SHASTA

The Mount Shasta area of ~~Washington~~ *California* state is the Epcot Center of sacred sites. The mountain emits such a strong energy pattern that satellite photographs show an atmospheric hole over its peak similar to the one found over Sedona, Arizona. The spirit of place of the site is multi-faceted, due to the internal activity of the mountain. Mount Shasta pushes and pulls, charges and draws energy from all around. The effect is dazzling. Standing 14,162 feet above the Cascade foothills, Shasta is considered a dormant volcano, in spite of the constant geological activity going on at any given hour.[1] Dormant, in this case, means the mountain is not oozing lava. The five glaciers that surround Shasta work constantly to mold the mountain to their liking. A secondary peak, Shastina, rises 12,000 feet from the west slope of Shasta.

What could be said about Shasta could fill an entire book. The first thing you notice about the mountain is how it stands out in such sharp contrast to its surroundings, like a single trophy in a showcase. There are steam vents, hot and cold springs, purification sites, electrical centers, and even caverns nearby that have been used by Native Americans for hundreds of years as sacred centers. A comparison of sites is most impressive, as it shows the varied ambiance of the region.

Photo by Tom Snyder

Mount Shasta's energy frequencies often cause anomaly light energy to appear around its summit.

On the slopes of Shasta is Panther Meadows, a very strong purification site that has been the subject of debate for some years regarding the morality of its capital development. Both in the past and recently, this site has been a place where people gather to perform sweat lodge and purification ceremonies. The intense purification of steam and heat within the lodge mimics what is going on inside the mountain. The cozy darkness of the lodge is almost maternal, and stirs up the goddess side of our spirit. The ceremony directs itself to the physical and spiritual cleansing of an individual,[2] as does the mountain.

Nearby, Shasta Caverns also has the ability to draw us back into the womb. The caverns are located about 2,000 feet above sea level, deep within the earth, 800 feet above the shores of Lake Shasta. The flowstone deposits of marble and limestone create an evocative gallery of artistic stalagmites and stalactites within the caves. The humidity in the caverns is about ninety-five percent, with an average temperature of fifty-eight degrees, a natural air-conditioned atmosphere used by the Wintu Indians hundreds of years ago.[3]

Looking up from the foothills at Mount Shasta could provide the sacred site explorer with some delightful experiences. Because of the strong geophysical forces at work within and about the mountain (especially during dry spells), different kinds of lights have been seen

Photo by Tom Snyder

Mount Shasta Caverns maintain an average 58 degrees. The caverns were used as a refuge and sacred site by the Wintu tribe of northern California.

on and around its peak. Sometimes these natural phenomena have been mistaken for UFO activity. This is not to say all the strange stuff that happens around Mount Shasta can be neatly swept under a scientific rug. It cannot. For those of you that are UFO enthusiasts, Shasta is a busy place you might want to check out. Just be aware that the mountain exhibits strong frequencies that create light shows. What you think you see is not always what you get, and vice-versa, on this mountain! On a clear night the mountain's visibility could be described as extreme. No matter if you are standing on Shasta's peak or resting in the foothills, the sky show is always a delight, whether it is lit up or not.

All around the Shasta region there are extinct and dormant volcanos, cinder cones, volumes of artesian springs, sacred caves, and mystical caverns, each with its own personality and character. Because of the energy at these sites Mount Shasta has been considered a sacred mountain throughout the history of the west. Its dominant characteristic is its versatile power, a power that seems to get stronger every day. As the Ring of Fire we so precariously sit upon dictates the fate of the Pacific, Shasta adjusts her energies to compensate for the ebb and flow of the earth's inner mantle. For now, the mountain has given us access to its energy centers. I have no doubt this will change in the future, as did the centers of power on Mount St. Helens after the explosion. Shasta is not extinct, only dormant, waiting for the right time to express magnificent power. Until then, the pristine meadows, graceful slopes, and isolated beauty of the mountain will continue to provide a haven for those who seek sanctuary from the world that lies at its feet.

CHAPTER 16

THE ANASAZI TRAIL

The Anasazi Trail is not really a trail at all, but the term used to describe a network of ruins belonging to the Anasazi civilization, the forefathers of the Hopi. The ancestors of the Anasazi were the hunters and gatherers known as the Archaic, who roamed the region from 5500 B.C. to the beginning of A.D. Artifacts along the trail have been carbon dated as far back as 9,000 years ago, suggesting an even earlier occupation of this area than history records.

The Archaic/Anasazi culture began its evolution when agriculture and basket weaving were introduced. Around A.D. 700 the Anasazi left their pit houses to build stone pueblos consisting of dozens, sometimes hundreds of rooms. These structures are referred to as the cliff dwellings of the Southwest and are liberally scattered throughout the region.[1]

Somewhere between 1270 and 1300 a drought finished off what was left of the Anasazi cliff dwellers and forced a migration to the southern Arizona plateaus and east toward the Rio Grande. Along with the migrations that sometimes took several generations to complete came a gradual change of lifestyle. By the time the Navajo arrived from the north the cliff dwellings had been abandoned. The Navajo never occupied the ruins. They said the spirits of the previous inhabitants protected the ghost dwellings and they feared them. Anasazi is popularly translated today as meaning Ancient or Wise Ones. The Navajo coined the phrase and according to them the name means "Enemy Ancestors."

Today, the history and early culture of the Anasazi can be found among many of the Pueblo tribes including the Hopi, Zuni, Tiwa, and Santa Domingo of the Southwest. Legends and traditions are passed on

Photo by Bernyce Barlow

Tuzigoot Ruins in the Central Corridor region of Arizona were passed on from the Anasazi to the Sinaqua. Approximately 225 people occupied this site in the mid-1200s.

Photo by Bernyce Barlow

An Anasazi granary ruin in the San Juan basin. Dried fruits, seeds, corn, and flour were stored in these cliffs high above the river. Grain tenders kept animals away from the storage area.

through dances, ceremonies, and festivals, kept alive by tribes whose ancestry can be traced back to the Anasazi. After spending time among the ruins, it is a wonderful feeling to experience a kachina dance or a greased pole event at one of the reservations, putting into perspective the advanced spiritual and colorful culture of the Anasazi.

At certain ruins like Wupatki, Chaco, and Tuzigoot you can view the ball courts that were used by the ancients for a very serious ball game. The story of the ball courts is told in the Mayan *Popol Vuh*, a story of two sets of twins who disturbed the Lords of Death of the underworld with their ball game. The Lords of Death had the first twins killed, burying one in the ball court floor of the Underworld and decapitating the other twin so his head would serve as a reminder to all, "do not disturb."

As the daughter of an Underworld Lord walked past the head, it spat on her, causing her to become pregnant. She gave birth to the second set of twins who defied the Lords through a series of trials. The legend ends with the twins tricking the Lords of Death into sacrificing themselves by promising them they would be resurrected, which of course they were not. The ball game represents the contest between good and evil, life and death.

Codices show teams of from two to eleven men that played for life and death stakes. Nobles often played against hero war prisoners. The ball was solid rubber weighing around forty pounds; a direct hit could be deadly. The ball games were an important part of the Anasazi culture and religion. The courts remain silent now but their ruins act as a reminder that the forces that were played out over and over again along the Anasazi Trail are still with us.[2]

As we travel along the trail, there are all kinds of sites to be discovered, with fairly complex sets of spirit of place. Some of the most intriguing are the solstice or observation sites found at most of the larger ruin areas. The architects of Hovenweep National Monument on the Colorado/Utah border spent a lot of time and energy getting the dimensions of their structures just right. At Hovenweep Castle, the doorway and portals of D Tower ingeniously mark the winter and summer solstices as well as the fall and spring equinoxes. At the Holly Group, under a sandstone ledge is a series of pictures etched into the wall that illustrate the summer solstice by shafts of light connecting the pictures. Obviously, the Anasazi recognized immediate planetary cycles and incorporated them into their daily lives and religion.

Another solstice site, the Fajada Butte Sun Dagger, is located among the spectacular ruins of

Photo by Bernyce Barlow

Eagle Point Pow Wow. Native Americans in traditional clothing perform traditional dances.

Chaco Canyon. Slabs of rock have been perched in front of a spiral symbol and a small slit between the slabs allows the sunlight to pierce the spiral in its center on the morning of the summer solstice. The site also marks the winter solstice and the moon equinox phases when the dagger pierces different sections of the spiral. The Sun Dagger is not open to the public, but more information about it can be obtained from the Chaco cultural center.

The breathing caves found along the Anasazi Trail are a different kind of sacred site, similar to those found at the base of Mount Taylor in New Mexico or at Wupatki in Arizona. Under the right conditions, the song of these caves can be heard many miles away. The negative ion-rich cool air that rushes to the surface from these enchanting caverns acts like a natural air conditioner for those above ground. These breathing caves were considered sacred by the Native Americans, not only for their unusual geological characteristics but for the atmosphere they create which triggers altered states.

There are also a number of underground springs in the Four Corners region, where Arizona, Utah, Colorado, and New Mexico meet, that go hand in hand with the breathing caves found there. The caverns were created by the subterranean springs when they ran closer to the surface. These springs keep up a regular ebb and flow that is actually tidal—curious considering how far from the ocean they are. The spirit of place at both the breathing caves and the underground springs found near or beneath them is a spiritual breath of fresh air.

The Anasazi Trail is one of the most spectacular collections of ancient ruins in America. In the Four Corners region alone, there is approximately one site per every ten square miles. The area is a treasure chest of archaeological and cultural riches comparable with the ruins of Central America and Europe.

Try to imagine yourself walking among the ruins of the ancestors of our country. In your mind's eye, you see on a sandstone wall a meticu-• lously painted figure, depicting the clan or tribe the artist belonged to. You wonder about the artist. As you approach a sacred spring near the ruins, you can see an ancient community capturing the precious water emitted from the ground. You hear the laughter of children and the barking of camp dogs, yet there is no one around but a tourist or two and you. Such experiences are not uncommon along the Anasazi Trail because the psychic imprint left on the land is so powerful. All sense of time and place become distorted, and you become a part of the imprint as an exchange of memory happens between the spirit of place and yourself. This kind of encounter allows you to peek around the bend through cracks in time. It leaves a lasting impression.

As you travel the paths that once guided our ancestors to their destiny, keep in mind that their hearts and souls are still with us. They can be found beneath the wings of the eagles that soar over the Sun Temple at Mesa Verde or deep in the ground kivas of Chaco Canyon. The heart of the Anasazi civilization takes shelter in the cliff dwellings on Ute Mountain, Canyon de Chelly, and all of the hundreds of other dwellings and sacred sites throughout the region. You only have to be among the ruins for a short while before they take you full circle, back to a time when the spirit of the Southwest lived its life through the Anasazi, and the Anasazi lived their lives through the spirit of the Southwest.

 Within the canyons along the Colorado River there are long peaceful stretches of river, interspersed with white-water rapids. The area pictured is a half-day paddle downstream from Moab, Utah, in Canyonlands National Park.

Photo by Bernyce Barlow

Photo by Bernyce Barlow

 Montezuma's Castle, near Sedona, Arizona, is the last among a series of ruins along Beaver Creek. Check dams, field houses, and ancient irrigation channels can be explored along a six-mile stretch of Beaver Creek above the castle.

 Ruins at a sinkhole on the floor of Montezuma's Well, near the well's outlet, where a powerful energy flow is released. The ruins were occupied by the Anasazi, Hohokam, and Sinagua people from A.D. 600 to the 1400s.

Photo by Bernyce Barlow

Hawaiian petroglyphs depicting male and female figures.

Pele is said to be seen in the glowing lava that flows to the sea. Hawaiians call Pele the "builder of islands." They say she melts the rocks, then molds them into new land. This kind of lava is called *pahoehoe*.

Photo by Bernyce Barlow

Photo by Bernyce Barlow

 Hawaiian tikis facing Honauna Bay on the Kona side of the island of Hawaii stand guard, ensuring that no malevolent spirits harm this site.

Photo by Deb Olson

Photo by Bernyce Barlow

Boynton Canyon, the home of the grandmother spirit Kamalopukwia, Old Lady White Stone.

 Canyonlands National Park in Utah. Wilderness campers must compete with scorpions and tamarisk bushes (above) for sleeping space along the sandbars on the riverbank.

Photo by Bernyce Barlow

Scene in the Barker Wonderland area of Joshua Tree National Forest Southern California. This desert region is a haven for Big Horn sheep.

Photo by Doug Deutscher

The Lavenderia at Mission San Luis Rey, California. Rock-lined bathing pools are located above the brick-walled laundry area.

Photo by Bernyce Barlow

Photo by Cheyenne Rouse

Sacred ground at Chaco Canyon. The Navaho called this type of pillar rock a "prayer perch." Eagles nest on the tops of these pillars.

Photo by Jeff Johnson

The Mexican pyramid actually is a four-sided flat-topped polyhedron, whose platforms were used by the Aztecs for sacrifices and ceremony.

Photo by Bernyce Barlow

Rock art of the Anasazi/Hopi near the entrance to Boynton Canyon at Sedona, Arizona.

Photo by S. Veirs

Albino Redwood was called the "ghost tree" by Native American tribes.

Photo by John Piephorn

The Highway to the Sun in Glacier National Park, Montana, is considered a place of emergence, symbolizing the goddess side of nature.

CHAPTER 17

THE SACRED WATERS OF BIG SUR

Along an eighty-mile stretch of coastline, only accessible by the picturesque yet treacherous California Highway 1, is a place called Eden West, or Big Sur. This coastal region is considered one of California's most beautiful areas, which is no small claim considering the diverse and striking scenery of the state. Waterfalls spill a hundred feet over polished cliffs onto the sands of the Pacific and quiet coves with aquamarine water shelter a healthy sea otter population, as well as seal and frolicking dolphin. The redwood groves found in Big Sur are as grand as the hamlet's name, reigning like royalty over the forest. Such a place must be called magic, and indeed it is by anyone who has had the opportunity to fall under its spell. But there is more to Big Sur than its magic, much more!

The Esalen, Carmel, and Chumash Indians wandered this territory for hundreds of years before the Spanish missions imposed their will. The region was a Garden of Eden full of game, ripe fruits, seeds, timber, and fresh sweet water. The sea provided sea mammal pelts for warmth and trade, as well as all kinds of delicacies to eat. The weather was seasonable and the winter was forgiving. What else could a community need? The extraordinary beauty of the landscape was inspiring and the people were grateful.

Photo by Bernyce Barlow

Highway 1 along the coastline at Big Sur can be treacherous under the best of conditions. During the summer the highway is often fogged in and mudslides are common.

An appreciation for life in Big Sur still flourishes in the community not only among those who live there, but also in those who are just passing through. It is one of the endearing qualities that belongs to the spirit of place of the region that gets passed on just by being there. It is no wonder so many of the "heavies" of the intellectual, metaphysical, and artistic communities end up in Big Sur for a while.[1] The town thrives on this kind of energy and passes it on through some kind of cooperative eco-osmosis. When a place is unusually powerful due to ambiance, imprint, and geophysics, it can be life-changing, given enough time. Big Sur is such a place.[2]

There are a number of sites within the coastal community that should be mentioned although, in an area as sacred and charming as Big Sur, it is sometimes difficult to pick them out. From the myriad of sites with diverse personalities throughout this hamlet, when I am visiting, unless I am doing research, I frequently pick a site depending on my mood. I like to spend my mornings absorbed in the mist and quiet found within the redwood groves and watch wild turkeys roam along parts of the Big Sur river as the sun comes up. The first awakening sounds, however, are usually from the bluejays, who consider the redwood groves their home.

In the afternoons I like to study the geology of Big Sur. The region is crisscrossed by a number of faults and fissures that often break through the surface creating a therapeutic spring. Many of these springs are located in the Ventana Wilderness Area and are accessible by trail. A topography map of the Ventana region is a good investment if you plan on doing any exploring; many of the springs are shown on the map. Make sure you check in with the ranger station, as well. Ventana is called a wilderness area for a reason. I have seen some very pretty mountain lions up there, so please pay attention.

Another set of springs can be found in the Tassajara area and can be reached by a Ventana Wilderness trail or driven to by following Tassajara Road to its end. Tassajara Road is not exactly in Big Sur. From Highway 1 in Carmel (north of Big Sur), turn east onto Carmel Valley Road and travel a little over twenty miles to Tassajara Road (south). These springs have been well developed, unlike those found within the wilderness area, but their healing properties remain the same regardless of what the hallowed waters are captured in.

Hundreds of years ago the Native Americans who lived in this region sought out the natural springs of Big Sur to heal, purify, and rejuvenate themselves. One spring was revered above all the others. This spring is now referred to as Esalen Hot Springs, calling attention to the now extinct Native Esalen community.

Today, the hot springs have been well developed by the Esalen Institute, whose property they flow through. Massive stone tubs built in the 1960s now capture the healing waters, adding to the ambiance of the site. The stone tubs sit, precariously high, two thousand feet above the shoreline on a rocky cliff overlooking the ocean.

There is something about the baths that makes you want to savor the moment. Maybe it has something to do with hearing the Pacific crashing onto the rocks below, the rhythm of the waves, or the nurturing warmth of the healing waters. Perhaps it is the moonlight, the candlelight, or the sweet sage that gives the baths their air of mystique. More than likely it is the combination of energy and ambiance which continues to make the site so special.

The springs located on the Esalen property have also drawn the international attention of modern-day healers. Some feel the spot where the waters of Esalen meet the ocean is an extreme place of power—a place where a healer can journey to find balance—a portal, so to speak, for an inner pilgrimage. Native American history agrees with this belief, and continues to honor the sacred springs.

Photo by Bernyce Barlow

Both inland and coastal waterfalls carry the sacred waters of Big Sur to the ocean. This site brings to mind Never-Never Land.

There is one other site in Big Sur whose sacred waters I'd like you to visit if possible. The waterfalls located in the Julia Pfeiffer-Burns State Park are truly awesome. Because of the geology of the terrain along the coast of California and the incidence of small earthquakes and mud slides, this site is not always accessible. Trails sometimes need to be repaired or closed. Check with the ranger on duty about access to the waterfalls. One waterfall in particular always inspired me as it plunges from a rocky cliff into the Pacific ocean.

If there are kelp beds and calm coves when you visit Julia Pfeiffer-Burns State Park, there will also be sea otters close to shore. Watching these creatures dive for food is delightful! After they have found some sort of shellfish they will roll over and float on their backs (sometimes supported by a kelp bed), place the shell on their tummy, and crack it open with a hard rock. After a good meal the otters can be seen tending to or playing with their families, and lounging around the kelp beds catching up on local chatter with other otters.

There was a time when the entire sea otter population along the California coast was thought to be extinct, due to Native American and European fur exploitation. These delightful ocean friends are back, but as adorable as the otters may appear they are wild animals with spiked teeth and extremely sharp claws. Unlike their buddy the dolphin, otter like to keep some distance between themselves and members of the human family. Knowing what we now know about genetic survival imprints, who can blame them?

A big part of the spirit of place in Big Sur has to do with purging, renewal, and preservation. This spirit can be felt and seen everywhere. Here, the otter are protected, the few remaining redwoods are fought for, and the wild turkeys know they will never go hungry. It is a place where peace and healing can be found in the forests, along the river, on the beaches, in the springs, and beside enchanted waterfalls. Most things are in balance here. Even during a chilling winter storm, nurturing warmth can be found bubbling out of the coastal cliffs and ground springs.

Harmony is hard to come by these days. Earth's balance has been disturbed, causing some of her music to be off tune, but harmony can still be found in Big Sur. It is the type of harmony that absorbs everything it surrounds, like a well-tuned orchestra playing Mozart. Balance and harmony are the key to wellness, and what better place to seek peace than at a site where harmony can be found just a stone's throw from the highway, and in the hearts of the people who live there.

Photo by Bernyce Barlow

The coves at Big Sur near Esalen are now a haven for sea otter. These coves once harbored pirates and slave traders.

No sacred site story about Big Sur would be complete without mentioning the sacred mountain, Pico Blanco, better known as White Peak. The indigenous people of this area consider Pico Blanco the place from which their ancestors came. Pico Blanco rises from the Santa Lucia Mountains, as a backdrop to the Little Sur River, and has been a site of legend and lore for centuries. One of the most intriguing tales was told by the late Alfred K. Clark, an eccentric miner.

While Clark was in search of a silver mine, he said he came across some subterranean caverns in the Pico Blanco region that were connected to the Little Sur River, just north of Point Sur. The caverns contained a river, and teemed with troglodytes, stalagmites, and stalactites, artifacts such as grinding mortars, and scores of cave paintings representing mammoth elephants and saber-toothed cats. After the discovery of this subterranean world, Clark became reclusive and mysterious. Not until he was on his deathbed did he give an account of his discovery.

Big Sur's underground world has yet to be rediscovered, although native legend, local geology, and history support the probable existence of a site like this. Pico Blanco has an abundance of limestone, a mineral easily sculpted by the elements. Numerous earthquakes along the shaky California coast may have obscured or closed the caverns' entrance.

Big Sur lore also includes a modern mystery. The Bixby Creek Bridge, a single-span arch, is an architectural wonder, and the site of visions. It is said that every once in a while an old World War I ghost plane is seen flying under the bridge. Those who live in the area also report hearing the plane as it flies up the canyon after clearing the bridge's arch. This is an unnerving encounter for those who experience it.

But not as unnerving as bumping into an embodiment of the most famous Big Sur legend, the "dark watchers." The watchers, mentioned in John Steinbeck's story "Flight," are usually one of the first legends told about Big Sur. The watchers are shadowy in form, not solid but curiously human-like. Their origin is thought to be another world, be it planet or dimension, and their purpose is unknown. It is said that these forms are found throughout the Santa Lucia range, and their presence can be felt by those whom they are watching.

CHAPTER 18

LAKE TOPAZ: A SPIRIT OF PLACE STORY

I was first introduced to Lake Topaz, on the California-Nevada border, five years ago, via Highway 395. My initial feeling toward the site was not overwhelming. As a matter of fact, I was not at all impressed, but it did not take long for the spirit of place at Topaz to shake loose those first impressions and turn them into a story about a sacred site whose holy history, function, and personality rival the best in the West.

When I mention Lake Topaz to High Sierra enthusiasts, eyes roll. Comments like, "With all the beautiful lakes in the area, why Topaz? It is man-made, it is set in a barren, high-desert basin, and the winds blow through there like a banshee!" These kinds of remarks make me smile, because it is for these very reasons the area has remained fairly unpopulated and quite undocumented until now. So, after five years of undisturbed research, study, and the exceptional expertise of Topaz Ranger Ted E. Dailey, the details of the Topaz region can finally be told. This is the first published composite summary of that story.

Ranger Dailey's knowledge and love for this region was the catalyst that enabled me to document this site with a great degree of accuracy. This account, from both of us, took us to the tops of golden mountains that hold the Archaic peckings of 9,000 years past, to hunting grounds, tool-making sites, goat blinds, rock quarries, ancient campgrounds, and crawling on our bellies into sacred caves. Because these sites have not been excavated or disturbed, Ranger Dailey and I have chosen not to expose their exact locations, but I did get some interesting photographs. The pothunters who raid historic sites, stealing and selling artifacts from sacred places, have made legitimate researchers cautious and protective, and until the tribal councils decide what they want done with the excavations, we must remain a bit obscure on a couple of the sites. In our own research, when an artifact was found, the place was marked and recorded, and the object was replaced after study as a sign of respect. If you visit there, please respect the spirit of place at Topaz.

Topaz was not always a high-desert alkali basin. At one time it was quite fertile, like a marshland, as were many of our western deserts. Standing on top of Wild Oat Mountain, look down on the lake and visualize a prehistoric zone where the lake now stands. Although Topaz is a man-made reservoir, it was constructed on a dry alkali lake bed which at one time was full of water, just as the lake is today. As time passed, the marshes dried up and volcanic activity changed the personality of the

Photo by Bernyce Barlow

The mouth of a sacred cave at Lake Topaz appears in the lower right corner of this photo. Note the spiral figures (center) and animal (upper left) painted on the stone outcropping.

Photo by Bernyce Barlow

Lake Topaz, on the California–Nevada border is on the North American Flyway. Migrating birds stop here to feed on the area's abundant resources.

land. During these changes humans began to occupy the region—some say 20,000 to 30,000 years ago, during the Bering Strait migrations. Ranger Dailey calculated one petroglyph site above the lake to be about 9,000 years old, placing its origin to the Archaic People.

Moving up on the Topaz time line, bits and pieces like chert arrowheads, obsidian chippings, and an occasional tool found in a nearby quarry (tucked into the hills in back of the water tower) link the site to a continuous hunting history. Where there is water there is life, and the Topaz region was teeming with it. Under the waters of the lake (built in 1921) are remnants of sheep blinds, trenches dug into the ground and covered with brush whose purpose was to first capture, then herd the wild game that fell into the ditches. Some miles to the southeast there are similar blinds built to catch rabbits.

Before this modern lake was formed, the pristine Walker River flowed through the site, supplying the native people with a generous amount of fresh water. Topaz is in the heartland of the High Sierras and a half-day hike will bring you to dense pine forests where more game species can be found. The people who occupied this region had a varied menu from which to chose, due to the close proximity of many ecozones, so they camped continuously here. One would be hard-pressed to find any land around the lake that was not used one way or another by the ancient people who called this their home.

Through the centuries many nations have passed through this area, including the Paiute, Shoshone, and Hopi. Ranger Dailey and I found conclusive evidence of these visits when we explored sacred caves in the area. To be fair, do not set out on foot to find these caves (they are thirty minutes by Jeep from Topaz and well protected). The cave site is truly spectacular and it took me some time to settle down enough so that I could focus on what I was supposed to be doing—documenting the caves. It was as if the spirit of place caught me off guard with its power and set me reeling.

The climb was straight up, but Ted and I had gotten an early start and were carrying enough water to fill up a camel. From the very beginning the energy was morphogenic—I had felt it many times at other sites and recognized it immediately. There was an electrical charge as well that became more apparent nearer to the top of the volcanic formation.

The rock art began to appear about one-third of the way up the peak we were climbing. At first there was just an occasional pecking, but closer to the top the recordings became more apparent and numerous. Images of suns, circles, snakes, lizards, horned toads, and sheep were everywhere, either pecked or painted in orange ochre on the cluster of boulders at the peak. There were also a few names and dates carved into the rocks (of some silver miners from the early 1800s) and on the back side of the formation there were two Chinese characters that represented an incline where the power of the Tiger and the Dragon meet. Wandering around the sacred grounds brought the realization that many different people had visited this site over the past few thousand years and that they knew of and recorded its power. This became clearly apparent when I stumbled (literally) over a rock I first thought to have a horned toad pecked into it. Upon further examination I found the carving to be

Photo by Bernyce Barlow

A shaman's story is told by the symbols of this petroglyph. Note the shaman's bird-like hands and feet, representing spiritual transformation.

that of Spider Woman, an image belonging to the Hopi. It was then with new eyes that I met the spirit of place of this sacred center, face to face.

It was time to document the caves. Compared to the outer entrance, the cave's walls were comparatively barren, with the exception of a lizard/man figure painted in ochre at the mouth of each cave opening. The ceilings were blackened from thousands of fires that had been built within the rock interior. There were places we had to crawl on our stomachs to explore and other places where a five-foot-tall person could stand erect. The caves were cozy and small and at the time of exploration we were sharing them with some critters with whom we made a pact. Under those cramped conditions the last thing we wanted was to run into a territorial skunk or badger. To our relief, there were no in-house confrontations.

With the photographs of lizard/man safely recorded on camera, I excused myself from the cool but dusty interior of the caverns and continued to explore the gallery of pictures surrounding the cave's entrance. Understanding the Hopi had been there, I looked for clan signatures and found them in abundance, next to the hunting records of the Paiute, which were next to the fertility symbols of another nation with a Shoshonean-based language that I couldn't identify. It was a most enchanting day, full of wonder and pleasant surprises everywhere I looked. I wanted to stay at this site, build a fire in the cave, and look out over the valley floor at twilight, but when it was time to go, Ted and I knew it. We received a gentle nudge from the spirit of place and took the hint. We followed a game path down the side of the peak which took us over the top of a lichen-covered mesa, then gradually down to the valley floor and back to my Jeep. Once again the region had left me with a sense of enlightenment and delight!

Back at the lake, my attention returned to the present, giving me the opportunity to focus on the Topaz of today. I grounded myself from the cave experience just as the sun was going down. A couple of pelicans swooped along the shoreline to catch a mouthful of dinner as I watched the sunset. Pelicans and other bizarre birds hang out at Topaz during their northern migrations because Topaz is on the North American flyway, making it a bird watcher's paradise.

In addition to the birds, trout, bear, mountain lion, skunk, badger, beaver, deer, rabbit, muskrat, packrat, and wild horses inhabit the hills surrounding Topaz. A couple of times a year the lake is shut down to visitors while sheep and cattle drives take place. It is like a page out of Western America's history books come to life. There are cowboys a'whooping and a'hollering, dogs barking, livestock kicking up dust, and cutting horses from the finest of quarterhorse lines dodging in and out of the herd, bringing in the strays. One really gets a feel for the West when the drives are in full swing. The sheep and cattle are usually brought down in the spring for sale or to summer over in the Lake Tahoe area. The rangers at Topaz never really know when the drives will take place until they receive a phone call from the trail boss who says, "We will be there in a few hours; please close the roads." This is the rangers' favorite time of year.

My favorite time at Topaz is the summer nights. A walk around the lake at 10:00 P.M. is like being in another world. There is a stillness that blankets the lakeshore but does not quiet the soul. Being so high up in the Sierras, where 12,000-foot mountains rise from lake level, one cannot help but feel a little closer to heaven. This is especially true at Topaz where planets jump out at you, satellites whiz by, and the constellations are dimmed by the brightness of the stars. To watch a mountain lion prowl the ridges above the lake, beneath the light of Sirus and a full moon, is to see Gaia as the romantic she is, stealthy, powerful, and graceful. Sometimes these night lights are so bright you can write by them.

As you can see, Topaz snagged my heart. Not bad for a site which upon first introduction I did not like even a little—but I kept coming back, year after year, invited by the spirit of place, until after a while the site became part of my dreams. When this happened I was shown the things I was to be aware of, document through photography, write about, and not write about. The spirit of place became my friend, as well as an exceptional guide. Now, when I sit on top of Wild Oat Mountain, I no longer see a void, barren, high-desert basin—instead I see a treasure chest full of ecstatic knowledge that links me not only to the past but to my future as well. The Earth is full of gems like Topaz, it's just a matter of holding them up to the sky to expose their true nature. In your explorations, if you come to a wild oat mountain where all the colors of the sun and moon seem to meet, you probably have found Lake Topaz.[1]

Author's Note: The cave site is now under the watchful eye of the Washoe tribe. Technical and unabridged documentation of this site will be registered with the Walker River Irrigation District, Nevada. Complete documentation includes statistics involving the nomenclature, input, and output of the lake's water volume, regulation equipment, pump house history, and impact of flood and drought conditions to the surrounding valleys fed by the lake.

CHAPTER 19

CHILD NEST ROCK

W hat follows is the first documentation of a site that Ranger Ted Dailey and I checked out one blistering July afternoon. We were actually on our way back from another site we had been documenting when Ted got what he describes as a compelling urge to return to a rock he had previously come across some years ago during a geological survey. If it had been anyone else, I would have reneged, but I have learned to respect Ted's instincts when it comes to sacred centers. Upon arrival we both had strong impressions at the site that stayed with us for a week. My initial research revealed the site had a name, Child Nest Rock. Driven by instinctive curiosity, Dailey took it from there. His study is recorded as follows, exclusively for the readers of this book.

Documentation of Child Nest Rock
by Ted Dailey

The state of Nevada lies mostly within the confines of the Great Basin, a huge and inhospitable land, a desert of grand and seemingly endless proportion, some 200,000 square miles consisting of about ninety valleys separated by mountains, a geographic system known to geologists as basin and range.

Thus, this system of valleys and ridges, basin and range becomes the Great Basin because all precipitation drains not to the sea but to the lowest point of each individual valley, so that the evaporation either from the ground surface or lake surface accounts for all the drainage. Rainfall averages between five and ten inches per year, but because of the climate little of this can be used by the plant population. Dry air, hot sun, and frequent hot winds contribute to a fast evaporation rate. Because of the lack of drainage, the Carson River, as an example, flows into the Humbolt sink and disperses over the land where the sun does its work.

Yet, in this sere and seemingly hostile environment, men and women have lived continuously for some 10,000 years. They formed the Desert Culture, evidence of which can be found throughout the Great Basin, sometimes in such spectacular form as the Sand Cave near Fallon, Nevada, where a rich trove of implements from everyday life was excavated by archaeologists. Mostly, however, the travels of the early People are marked by the appearance on the desert floor of a few flakes from stone tools, or in rare cases by a petroglyph or pictograph, symbols or pictures pecked into the rock or painted with locally available materials such as ochre. Recently, I camped at such a site, scant miles from the old Emigrant's Trail. There is a feel and magnetism about this place which transfers to the interested observer. The local people call this site Child Nest Rock.

Photo by Bernyce Barlow

Ranger Ted E. Dailey of Topaz Lake prepared the first documentation of Child Nest Rock.

Photo by Oz Johnson

The crone rock formation at Child Nest Rock marks this birthing site of desert culture children. Fifteen small graves are clustered near this rock.

Rising from the middle of a desolate plain, surrounded by distant mountains, rugged and sharp in the clear high desert air, rising like a stegosaurus from a sand swamp, is Child Nest Rock. The tail, extending due east, swells into the mighty body with upthrust slabs of basalt culminating in a rocky cliff face where the head might have been. It is the only feature on this flat landscape, and it draws the eye immediately, the way a rainbow will stand out in an otherwise gray sky. This rock, covered in green and orange lichen, once attracted the attention of the Archaic People as well, because they have left behind their sign. Scattered around this lonely, isolated outcrop are chert and obsidian leavings from the manufacture of stone tools, bifaces, gravures, and arrowheads. The People camped here in prehistoric times.

There are other historic remains overlying the Neolithic debris: weathered beer cans with bullet holes, unidentifiable bits of plastic and paper trash that present-day man cannot seem to avoid leaving behind. There is also nineteenth-century trash rusted-out, soldered-together tin cans, pieces of pearlized or purple glass, signifying the visitation of prospectors or miners. None of the debris detracts from the presence of Child Nest Rock. It is a evidence that people have been here very recently and have not treated the site with much respect.

Approaching Child Nest Rock, one is struck by the apparent lone-liness of this outcropping, rising up out of a basin floor covered with stunted sage, rabbitbush, and creosote. The sandy soil crunches underfoot, until you step onto a collapsing ground squirrel burrow and sink a couple of inches. Here and there are small clumps of sand grass (also known as Indian rice grass)—that very nutritious and important part of the regional Archaic diet, right up until the People became known as the Paiute Nation or the Numa, from whence we get the oral information concerning the harvesting and preparation of native resources. Lizards abound and overhead, high overhead, wheel two turkey vultures, soaring on the thermal currents, their fleshy, naked heads swiveling in search of food. Heat rises in shimmering waves from the desert and from the dark stone of Child Nest Rock. I began my exploration.

Climbing to the top of the outcrop, there are several pack rat nests and in one obvious place a perch point for a bird of prey, the rocks below its outlook stained white with guano. There is a small rock-tilt, affording a coyote some degree of shelter, and then I find at the very top, a sheltered place, a nest, large enough to lie down in and contem-plate the heavens; or a place to give birth to a child, or a place in which to die. It is a natural shallow bowl about the size of a human being. I think about the name given to this rocky place in the middle of such a desolate area: Child Nest Rock—and wonder how far back in the deep-est mists of time this name originated.

Out of the nest, I climb down over the rough rocks, the stegosaurs' back, and circumvent the outcropping. It is there definite evidence of the People can be found; the chert stone cores and many flakes—evi-dence of tool making, possibly a camp, or a meeting place.

Ethnographers say that the Archaic People tended to hunt and gather in small family groups, traveling from harvest area to harvest area as the season dictated, with the women harvesting the plant life and the men hunting. They also say, based on their research, that there were sacred rituals involving the coming of age of both men and women, which were almost certainly long and elaborate. At the culmi-nation of these ceremonies, or at the end of the lengthy and lonely fasts, a vision would sometimes occur, a guiding spirit would appear, and the participant could then emerge into adulthood.

These incredibly hardy, intrepid, and courageous People were in complete contact with the land in which they lived. They knew to a day when to harvest the rice grass, when to dig the Sego Lily bulbs, and

Photo by Bernyce Barlow

Circular foundations are scattered throughout the Child Nest site, mute evidence that an ancient community once thrived there.

when the pinenuts were ready to gather. They knew where to hunt and to fish when the game was most plentiful and when the fish were spawning. At certain times of the year, they gathered in groups larger than family to harvest certain natural resources, such as in November when the mud hens were too fat to fly and could be easily collected and smoked or air dried for the winter: and when the rabbits could be driven through blinds by large numbers of people and then harvested.

These were also times when mates could be found, when feasts were held, when information was exchanged. These were a time of bounty, when such luxuries as rituals and rites could occur. I believe Child Nest Rock was a place of ceremonial significance deeply connected to the aboriginal People.

Wandering around the rock we found more and more evidence of human habitation. East of the Child's Nest was a men's encampment. Here were the flakes and stone cores from tool and arrowhead making. West of the outcropping the site was relatively barren of artifacts. On the south side of the rock there is a single petroglyph of a female fertility symbol, pecked into the rock near the ground. Near this lone petroglyph is an ancient rock circle, the probable foundation of a sweat lodge, dreaming circle, menses hut, or habitation from long ago.

We do not know a lot about the cultural level of these ancient People. We only vaguely understand, through the sciences, their history. The clearer story is told by the Nations and at the sites themselves. What we do know is that the People who used Child Nest Rock were high on the scale in their ability to survive, their reading of the land, and the use of natural resources. They not only survived, but even prospered in a hard place, earning a well-deserved respect. The encampment at Child's Nest Rock reminds us of this lesson through its spectacular Paleozoic form and Archaic spirit of place, a spirit I have been drawn to, and again will return to, because Gaia's presence rests there comfortably, quietly, and boldly as she does at the most sacred sites. It is a place to listen and learn.

Author's Note: Because the site is protected only by its anonymity and has not yet been excavated, Ranger Dailey and I both agree the exact location of Child Nest Rock should remain undisclosed. The location of the site is obscure, and located on private property. Most people would not have the opportunity to visit there whether they knew of its location or not, so we have done our best to bring Child Nest Rock to you.

CHAPTER 20

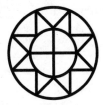

HAWAIIAN PETROGLYPHS

There is something mystical about the petroglyphs found scattered around the island of Hawaii. Figures and symbols etched into lava fields, lava tubes, and caves recount prehistoric details we would otherwise have missed, a sacrifice or a political coup, a birth or a game tally—details recorded by individuals that tell the story of an island and its people. Perhaps that is what makes the petroglyphs so intriguing.

The word "petroglyph" comes from the Greek words *paetros*, meaning stone, and glyphe, meaning carving or image. There are quite a few schools of thought on the origin and meaning of Hawaiian petroglyphs. Some feel many of the petroglyphs were just doodles made by the islanders as they traveled around the island, leaving what amounts to be a signature at a site. Others feel the pictures express the only form of writing known to the Hawaiians and represent more than just pictures and signatures. These experts feel the petroglyphs represent recorded events left by individuals at specific times. A third theory argues the symbolic meaning of the petroglyphs lies within the inner sanctions of the Hawaiian priesthood and will not be eagerly passed on outside the culture for strangers to exploit.

With so many theories to study, it makes it difficult to intimately connect with the rock art of Hawaii. We know a great deal about the

Photo by Bernyce Barlow

Lava fields on the island of Hawaii are etched with hundreds of petroglyphs. The image above was used repeatedly.

petroglyphs of the Southwest because the symbology has been kept intact by the more traditional tribes. The very nature of Hawaii has been integrated by so many cultures, helping to bury the original culture beneath an avalanche of migrating foreign customs.

Despite the melting pot of customs Hawaii has become today, the essence of the island has not changed and some of the petroglyphs no doubt do represent sacred symbols known only to the elite. Some of the petroglyph sites may dramatize the importance of the spoken word that was so significant to the Hawaiians. The islanders lived by the edict, "if you say it meaningfully it will come to pass."

From its history to its law, much of the early Hawaiian culture was based on the spoken word. Kaunas would give long sing-song speeches that rhymed, mostly praising and describing the forces of nature, to please the gods. If a prisoner failed to find the right rhyme or cadence when speaking to the courts, he would be killed on the spot. The spoken word was sacred to the Hawaiians, and to etch these words or symbols onto a lava canvas would empower the word and the artist. This is, of course, yet another school of thought concerning the origin and meaning of the petroglyphs.

As you travel around the island you will find a variety of petroglyphs. The majority depict weapons, tools, animals, people, fish, and boats. It is easy to get wrapped up in the meaning of the petroglyphs, but bottom-line interpretation is an individual hypothesis, at best.

A good place to appreciate these rock carvings is in the petroglyph fields between the Waikaloa and Mauna Lani resorts on the sunny, eastern side of the island. There, various types of figures are carved into reddish-brown lava fields. The Mauna Lani fields require a short hike through a snag forest straight out of Monty Python's Flying Circus, but at the end of the trail is a spectacular lava field that is home to hundreds of carvings. The Waikoloa fields are more scattered along a trail that skirts a nearby resort. Both sites are worth a visit. Occasionally, if you closely explore the island, you will find carvings on individual rocks or on the walls of sacred Hawaiian caves or waterfalls. These petroglyphs are probably the type that are meaningful to the priesthood of the island. No matter where you find these intriguing links with the past, you will marvel at the mystery left behind in the petroglyphs of the ancient Hawaiian culture.

CHAPTER 21

WUPATKI

L ooking at the ruins of Wupatki, it is hard to imagine why anybody would want to settle in this area. The land is harsh and desolate, displaying extreme temperatures, above and below zero, throughout the year. Winds bite and dust storms blind the unfortunate traveler who visits Wupatki during one of these turbulent occurrences. What vegetation does exist has a hardy nature, clinging to gullies and rivulets carved by runoff erosion. Summer brings searing heat, with little relief until nightfall. Water evaporates before it hits the ground—including the sweat off your brow. With this description in mind, how was it this unlikely region became a center for a mixture of peoples over thousands of years?

Archaeological finds dating back 11,000 years give proof that this area was inhabited early. Chipping and tool-making grounds have been found dating to 500 B.C. along the Little Colorado River bordering the park district as well as sacred sites that appear to be of Anasazi origin. The A.D. 1064 eruption of nearby Sunset Crater set in motion a 200-year-long volcanic tantrum, burying beneath cinders, ash, and sand much of what we need to put together all the pieces of the Wupatki puzzle. Pre-eruption sites are nearly nonexistent, so the bulk of information we do have on Wupatki has been accumulated from after the eruption.[1]

George H. H. Huey

Starting in 1064, Sunset Crater continued to erupt for 200 years. Its final burst of activity in 1250 tossed particles of iron and oxydized sulphur onto the rim of the crater, giving the volcano its red-orange color and name.

The Sinagua People left us clues to study about the area. They developed Wupatki into a cultural trade center dating from after the Sunset Crater eruption until well into the 1300s. Around 1150 the Sinagua civilization began to expand and reached a certain purity within its culture. Agricultural methods had been learned from the nearby Hohokam. Lucrative trade was set up with the Kayenta and Winslow Anasazi, the Cohonina, and the Prescott tribes. Rain was increasing and the volcano had fertilized the earth and provided a mulch that prevented the ground water from evaporating too quickly. Farming was successful, trade was brisk, and for some time all was well with the Sinagua. We know this because of the wonderful ruins of Wupatki. After the 1300s, as the tribe adopted many of the customs and cultures of neighboring tribes, they assimilated themselves into extinction.

A walk through the visitor's center of the Wupatki Monument reveals a rich history of trade and religion. Outside of the center are the ruins of Wukoki and Wupatki. Here it becomes most evident that the Sinagua culture was connected through assimilation of customs to the ancient cultures of the past. The ball court near the ruins is a prime example; the ball court game can be traced back to Mesoamerican influence. The Hohokam tribe probably introduced the game to the Sinagua.[2]

There is an enchanting amphitheater near the ruins whose purpose is not really known, although there are plenty of theories to fill in the blanks. For the more adventurous, there are check dams, tanks or natural catch basins that have been dammed, small field houses, and ancient garden plots to explore. These are found on the Antelope Prairie in the western part of the monument. Also within the monument boundaries are the Kayenta Anasazi ruins of Citadel and Lomaki, and the Sinagua ruin of Nuvakwewtaqa nearby on Anderson Mesa.

For those interested in petroglyphs, Wupatki is a playground. There are a number of private and public sites that display a cross-representation of many cultures. A wonderful collection of Anasazi rock art can be found near the Crack-in-Rock ruins. There are also fine examples of Hopi rock art depicting clan symbols and migration marks. The petroglyphs represent a myriad of subjects including bugs, birds, migration, rain, hunting, fertility, and spirit guides. The monument is a stone library for those with an eye for prehistoric news.

One of the joys of Wupatki is that it allows the visitor to see how a complete community was structured in ancient times. From the ball courts and the amphitheater we can put together a picture in our mind of hundreds of people coming together for sports and public meetings. We can follow the ancient irrigation ditches to the small one-room field houses that gave the farmer shelter from the sun or wind and a place to sleep during the busy harvest season. Cemeteries and solar observation spots add mystique to Wupatki, as do the remains of buried parrots and exotic items recovered from these types of sites. From the wealth of data left behind by the early People of this district we can almost reach back through time and touch the civilizations who developed this region into an outpost of cultural exchange.

It is also interesting to note the numerous geological phenomena in or near the monument. Some of the breathing caves or blowholes that are scattered throughout this region are located in the park.[3] There are many legends concerning these caves that differ in storyline depending on whom you are talking to. The breathing caves can be heard for miles around when the conditions are just right, not to mention the negative ionized air that is sent rushing through them. Some breathing caves in the Four Corners area have been clocked at 30 M.P.H. under certain circumstances. In an area known for its unmerciful heat, these blowholes are the naturally perfect air conditioning units of the desert. They are also native sacred sites where many an ecstacy state has been sought out and reached due to the unusual characteristics of the spirit of place at the blowholes themselves.

As you can see there is more than meets the eye at Wupatki. What first appears as a barren, desolate outpost becomes a hub of interaction for the imagination of the sacred site explorer. At one time in history this village was a place where many tribes exchanged goods and traditions in peace, an unprecedented occurrence among the People of the Southwest at that time.[4] Wupatki offers us the privilege to explore a fairly intact piece of history, enriching our present views of the past with accuracy. If the land was more hospitable the endearing remnants of this outdoor museum's history would be lost to housing tracts and condo units. Instead, Wupatki has been left alone to brace itself, protected by the acrimonious elements of the region against the more devastating results of modern civilization. Although the spirit of place of Wupatki seems extreme, it is this very quality that has protected the magic of the ruins from disappearing. Today, the magic of Wupatki remains for those willing to seek out the desolate galleries tucked into the nooks and crannies of the monument. The search will not only take you back in time but will bring time to you, and that is where you will find the true spirit of Wupatki.

THE GODDESS

Chapter 22

Goddess Sites

Fern Canyon is one of the sacred sites located along the coast of Northern California. Steep cliffs, a stone's throw apart, compete with the redwoods for a piece of the sky, making the canyon more like a grotto than a forest. Thousands of sword fern cover the canyon walls, leaving the floor to diversity. There a fresh water creek finds its way to the ocean a few hundred yards west and sun-shy wildflowers bloom, adding a splash of color to a verdurous background.

The ambiance of Fern Canyon changes from season to season, sometimes from day to day, depending on her mood. She is not fickle like some canyons, nor is she fragile. She is, however, sensitive. The spirit of place within her canyon walls speaks in whispers and one must listen closely to hear. Her presence is everywhere. When the coastal fog finds its way into the grotto, she can be seen as slender fingers of mist bringing precious water to the thirsty giants in her womb. During the harsh storms of winter, the canyon's womb protects what is hers from the ravages of the season and gives birth in spring to yet another cycle of life.

The spirit of place at Fern Canyon teaches valuable lessons about the goddess side of our lives. We all came from the womb, but few of us remember that experience. To spend time in the canyon cradled among the redwoods and ferns brings us back to the nurturing safety of our origin and perhaps reteaches us what we have forgotten.

There are other sacred sites, goddess in spirit of place, that teach different aspects of the nature of womanhood. Mount St. Helens in the state of Washington is an excellent example. She is called the Little Sister mountain by the tribes of the Northwest. Mount Rainier is her grandfather.

Before Little Sister threw her tantrum, she was as proper and pristine as any mountain could be, a beauty of a peak with sweet streams and crystal clear lakes. For three months before the major explosion Little Sister stomped around and blew off enough steam to get everyone's attention. When she had it, she flexed it. Legend tells us that when Little Sister cries, Grandfather will answer. I believe he will.

There is more to the spirit of place on Mount St. Helens than an angry child. If we listen to the tribes of the Northwest, they will tell us

Photo by Robert Firth

"Little Sister," Mount St. Helens. When Little Sister cries, Grandfather (Mount Ranier) answers.

that the mountain was tired of the pollution from the cities at her feet, and that she was hurt from having the trees stripped from her slopes. The birds and four-legged animals were losing their homes and the waters that came from the winter's snowmelt were now polluted. The salmon that once visited Little Sister no longer came and she was lonely. Her anger was justified, and being a small child, she just blew up!

After the eruption, life in the red zone (indicated on forestry and park service maps as an area considered unsafe for travel) was non-existent. I take solace in knowing that seven days before the major eruption on May 18, 1980, hundreds of animals left the mountain. Herds of elk and deer came down off St. Helens and successfully crossed Interstate 5 near Kelso. Big cats and beaver were also relocating themselves northwest of the mountain. Why some animals left and others stayed is a question that remains unanswered, but there is no doubt as to the devastation left in the aftermath of the eruption.

The spirit of place of Mount St. Helens is speaking to us in another tone now. It is quieter, softer—no longer warning us, but showing us what could happen if we do not stop ravaging the earth. The mountaintop remains a moonscape instead of a garden of Eden, a pile of rock rubble and ash instead of a forest. Is this something that could happen on a global scale if we do not change our ways? Little Sister says yes. Will we listen this time to this child goddess, or wait for her grandfather's answer?

We have examined two goddess spirit of place sites, both very different from each other. One the nurturing mother, the other the angry child, each having its own story to tell and, in St. Helen's case, to show. Not all goddess sites have such a universal message. Some sites are quite practical and possess a healing spirit of place for which, quite frankly, men do not have a need. That is not to say that men do not benefit from the healing energies of these sites. I know they do, just not in the same way a woman would.

Hudspeth County in western Texas is well known for its network of twenty-two artesian springs that for centuries have been used by Native Mexican and American tribes for healing, especially among women and medicine seekers.[1] A very strong spirit of place resides there at Indian Hot Springs. Developers have tried to turn the springs into a five-star resort many times, but development plans always seem to fail. It is as if the spirit of place of the springs will not consider compromise. It is a healing site, not a circus. The simple use is allowed for comfort but capitalistic gain from the site does not seem to be tolerated.

Photo by Bernyce Barlow

Adobe ovens at the Tiwa Reservation heat the pueblos during the cold winter months. The oven's womb-like shape is no coincidence—emergence and Mother Earth are common structural themes in pueblo dwellings.

I consider this site a very practical site for women, because its healing nature concerns itself with the cycles of a woman's life, from premenstrual to menopause. There are specific places a woman can sit along the string of wells where earth energies will help subdue menstrual cramps. Other springs aid in purification and internal cleansing, and others chase away melancholy. When combined, the mud, mosses, rocks, and energy fields provide a healing network that aids the goddess body in functioning.

Knowing this, a subtle message is passed on from Gaia to her sisters on the planet. She understands and has provided places all around the globe where women may come for healing and fellowship.

There is, of course, more to a woman than her body. The intricate system of mind and spirit, intuition, and survival makes a neat little package to unravel. With so much going on in a woman's life, it is sometimes difficult to find the time and energy to peel back all the layers to examine the individual aspects of womanhood in the pure light of goddess creation. There are sacred sites that can help to do just that.

Bell Rock in Sedona, Arizona is an excellent example of such a site. It is not a site one should approach to work out heavy problems. On the contrary, it is a site to celebrate womanhood and recharge. The child is easily released on Bell and an attitude of play and awe can quickly take over if you let it.

An exciting energy found on Bell Rock is the razor-sharp edge given to intuition, a well-developed skill most women possess in quantity. Bell Rock hones this skill quickly and flawlessly, using her powerful electrical upsurge[2] as a whetstone. Coming off the rock, both men and women find their intuitive abilities sharpened and

Photo by Bernyce Barlow

Bell Rock near Sedona, Arizona is an extraordinary place to find and experience the joyous side of your inner child.

keen, but for women, whose intuitive powers are a given, the experience can be quite powerful.

There are many other sacred sites scattered throughout the world whose purpose specifically benefits or honors women. Some are well-known, such as the temples of Delphi in Greece or the fertility sites on Ring Mountain near Tiberon, in central California. There are other sacred sites quietly tucked away on the planet that are waiting for recognition.

I encourage the acknowledgment of goddess sites and the understanding that the *genus loci* of a site is sometimes feminine—a natural conclusion if you think about it. I also encourage the exploration of such sites for both men and women, not only the well-known sites but those that have a personal flavor for an individual.

Gaia is a woman. The key to understanding her is both individual and universal. Where better to explore her character than at the same gender sites she provides for us? No matter if she is teaching us about the nurturing spirit of the womb, warning us of global disaster, sharpening our intuition, or healing our bodies; the mysteries of creation and procreation unfold in Gaia's presence.

If you want to feel womanhood, go to the places where the feminine is strongest—the sacred sites that both whisper and roar, the centers that collect and distribute Gaian energy, the sister sites that women have depended on since their conscious beginning and the sites to which men have gone to understand the feminine mystique for centuries. These goddess sites enhance our understanding of the planet and ultimately ourselves. They provide us with a place to gather to celebrate the goddess light in each of us, so that light may shine brilliantly through us all.

CHAPTER 23

EMERGENCE SITES

A common sacred theme among the tribes of the Southwest is emergence. There are several sites whose holy history recognizes this concept throughout the region. Although the locations of emergence sites may vary, their numinous significance is communal. They are centers that represent physical birth and spiritual rebirth. The Hopi tribe of Arizona tells us their ceremonial *kivas* represent Mother Earth. The small hole built into the floor of the kiva, the *sipapuni*, signifies the womb, and the ladder leading out through the roof of the kiva represents the umbilical chord leading to yet another emergence. During the ritual of *Wuwuchim,* the emergence legends of the Hopi are passed on to initiates seeking spiritual rebirth.[1]

Another type of emergence site can be found in the Sangre de Cristo mountain range above Taos, New Mexico. The Sangre de Cristos are the sacred mountains of the Tiwa tribe of New Mexico, and Blue Lake is their ceremonial place of emergence. At one time the tribe did not have private access to the site but in 1970 President Richard Nixon[2] signed a bill returning 44,000 acres of land, including Blue Lake, to the tribe. It is also interesting to note that the Great Sand Dunes near Alamosa are also considered a place of emergence for the Taos tribe.

Lakes, springs, and wells are often the location of an emergence site. West of Taos, Ojo Caliente, another legendary Tiwa site, hosts five different springs that have been used for their physical and spiritual properties for hundred of years. The springs are said to be the home of the grandmother of Poseyemo, a sacred spiritual figure of the Tiwa. The springs are also known as windows between the outer world and the place of emergence.[3]

Kiva ruins near Grants, New Mexico. Note the sipapuni.

The Tiwa reservation is occupied by traditionalists of the tribe. They travel annually to their symbolic emergence site at Blue Lake.

Visitors who come to Ojo Caliente usually do so for the healing properties found at the springs. Iron, sodium sulfate, lithia, soda, and arsenic are all part of the chemical composition of the water. The arsenic spring is the only one that can be found on the North American Continent. The only other known arsenic spring on the earth is found in Baden-Baden, Germany.[4] These springs are playfully dubbed the mother-in-law springs and are the subject of some rather cruel in-law jokes.

Montezuma's Well in Arizona is another good example of an emergence center. The well is a funnel-shaped limestone sinkhole, fifty-five feet deep and 368 feet across. It is fed a million and a half gallons of subterranean spring water daily and is the site of emergence of Kamalopukwia, the grandmother spirit of Boynton Canyon, and her grandson, Sakaraka, the first of the Yavapai "People." After the arrival of the grandmother and Sakaraka on this world others followed to settle the land outside of the well. The giant spring was kept a secret for many years from the Spanish who entered this region in the 1500s. It was a sacred site the Native Americans of the area did not want to reveal.

There is a fine network of ruins, irrigation channels, and check dams that were created to divert the waters of the well to a nearby community. Some of the earlier inhabitants of this area, the Hohokam and

Photo by Bernyce Barlow

Montezuma's Well is a fresh-water spring that is fed 1.5 million gallons of water daily. To Native Americans, this site continues to be the sacred emergence sit of Kamalopukwia and her grandson, Sakaraka.

later the Sinagua, first used the spring for irrigation and ceremonial purposes. Tribes entering the corridor at later dates added their own flavor to the site, making the well an archaeological treasure chest.

We have examined sites that are structurally symbolic of emergence such as kivas. Other places of emergence are set in natural environments such as at wells, springs, and lakes. There are ethereal sites that are connected to the spiritual comings and goings of the soul as well. Point Conception, above Santa Barbara, California, is considered the western door for newly arriving and departing souls by the Chumash Tribe. It is said that the eastern portal for these souls rests on Assateague Island off the coasts of Maryland and Virginia.[5] Although we physically cannot enter or submerge ourselves in these ethereal sites the energies found there represent a kind of emergence and can be tapped into spiritually.

Places of emergence that can be found worldwide exhibit a deep respect for the goddess side of nature. Mimicking the womb, these sites remind us of the process of birth, renewal, and awakening. The nurturing spirit of the earth is held in high esteem at these sites, especially as a symbolic mother whose desire is to spiritually ground her children in the ways of the creator.

Women who visit emergence sites say the spirit of place often reveals the inner symbology of mother and child. This age-old symbology can be physically traced around the globe, from the ancient residents of Egypt and Crete into the jungles of Panama.[6] The symbols act as a bridge between the conscious and subconscious. There are volumes of material by Joseph Campbell on the subject, if you are interested in the effects symbology has on the subconscious. As the symbols of emergence reach the deepest corners of the mind, men and women part company, for the symbols represent something only woman can achieve, birth. As a passionate contributor, the male psyche can observe and understand the symbols, but can rarely resonate them. That is why emergence sites affect women so profoundly.

On a personal note, you can find your own place of emergence. It may be a cave or a body of water that spiritually speaks to you. The Smith River in northern California is the place I have chosen in which to examine the spiritual side of my womanhood. I go there as often as I can to learn from the spirit of place at a particular pool of glacial green water. It is my place of emergence. I encourage you to seek your own place of power, a sacred site that you emerge from physically and spiritually renewed.

CHAPTER 24

LUNCH CREEK

On the Highway to the Sun, in Glacier National Park, a pristine brook, inspired by fire and ice, trickles through a glacial meadow forming Lunch Creek. The spirit of place at Lunch Creek lies in the magnitude of its destiny. There is a certain magic in watching the sun melt drops of glacial ice, to see the drops become a stream, then a river rushing toward the sea.

Lunch Creek is a goddess site that unveils herself for the sun. For a few short months her beauty can be admired, but most of the time she is cloaked by winter's snow. During the summer her ways are gentle and youthful, all the young flowers come out to greet her. Tender grasses and new moss grow as close to her as possible, for her energy is endearing. To look upon the tremendous glacier above Lunch Creek is like looking at raw power. The meadow and creek cushion the intimidating impact of the mountain on people. Lunch Creek welcomes you to stay when you might otherwise leave. She is, among other things, a gracious hostess.

The physics in the high meadows of the Rockies consist of a combined flow that imitates a positive electromagnetic vortex. This energy pattern is also found in Tibet and at Crater Lake, Oregon.[1] It is a wonderful energy pattern that feels like beauty. The electrical charge at Lunch Creek is like a feminine giggle coming from the site's spirit of place.

Photo by Bernyce Barlow

Lunch Creek is a sacred site of the Blackfoot Nation, and displays a playful energy during the summer months. Awe-inspiring beauty surrounds those who visit this site.

Avalanche Lake, on the "Going to the Sun Road," is the local water hole for the grizzly bears and mountain lions frequently seen in this part of Glacier National Park. Moose can often be spotted if the grizzlies and cougars are not around.

When you visit Lunch Creek, come prepared for quick changes in the weather. Although the creek is not fickle, the Rocky Mountains are! If you plan on doing anything serious at this site, forget it. The energy scrambles your brain. It makes you want to play, so dip your toes into the creek and look at bright pebbles polished by the water, meet little frogs and count butterflies with the spirit of place, because all too soon the holiday will end with the first snow. Lunch Creek will put on her cloak and quickly disappear into the winter season and will not return until the sun is again high in the sky.

CHAPTER 25

THE KILAUEA CALDERA

The Kilauea Caldera is said to be the home of Pele, the Hawaiian goddess of fire. As legend goes, Pele came to the Hawaiian islands to escape her sister, Na Maka O Kaha'i, the goddess of the sea. Pele started her journey on the island of Kawai digging into the earth with a great stick to make a home for herself. Although she dug very deep into Kawai, Na Maka always managed to somehow extinguish Pele's fire. Pele moved from island to island digging pits deep into the ground to protect her fires but she was always followed by Na Maka who would put them out.

Finally, Pele settled on the island of Hawaii and dug a deep pit into Kilauea, the site she now calls home. For now, this pit, called a caldera, protects the fires of Pele and it is here more than any other place that the spirit of Pele can be felt. Kilauea rises 22,000 feet from the ocean floor and stands approximately 4,000 feet above sea level.[1] It is a noble mountain home to a noble lady.

The Hawaiians call Pele the builder of islands and the destroyer of forests. They say she melts the rocks, then molds them into new land. At will, Pele destroys, then builds, depending on her mood. When she is particularly angry she will hurl rocks at her enemies and cover their bones with her molten flesh. Her spirit is strong and at times demanding, but Pele is also the mother of new land and is very protective of that which is hers. The rocks are her children, and to pocket even a pebble from the island will induce her wrath. Do not even think about it or you will get burned!

There are not as many heiaus near the caldera as one would think. The islanders understood the fiery goddess' moods and gave her plenty of space to vent her emotions. There was a heiau on Waldron Ledge and another where the observatory now stands on Uwekahuna Bluff. Both were used for sacrifice.

The physics of Kilauea is active and stimulating, if not a little heady. Beneath the caldera, a source deep in the Earth's mantle heats rocks until they become fluid. This molten substance is called magma. When magma flows from a volcano, it is called lava. The island of Hawaii sits upon a conduit that feeds the magma into the caldera. As long as the island remains over the conduit, Hawaii will continue to grow. Eventually, the magma source will be cut off as the island drifts to the northwest on the Pacific Plate.

Photo by Bernyce Barlow

From crater to sea, Pele, the builder of islands. In Hawaii, this type of lava called *pahoehoe* delicately folds into itself, creating an enchanting design.

Photo by Deb Olson

The caldera of Kilauea is the most recent home of Pele, the Hawaiian Fire Goddess. To remove any lava from this site is like inviting Pele to stalk you. The lava rocks are considered the children of Pele.

In twenty million years, the sheer weight of the island will cause it to submerge into the sea just as other islands in the chain have done. Despite the fiery nature of Pele, Na Maka always seems to win. Islanders say Pele is often destructive and angry because the constant battle with her sister is always in vain.

Pele is at her best at night when her face is aglow and radiant. To watch the red-orange lava flow gracefully down Kilauea's slopes is like watching a slow dance to the sea. Spirals and faces, angels and images, all glowing, flow and merge together to become something different farther down the path. The dance is elegant and seductively mesmerizing, as is Pele.

Pele represents the fiery side of womanhood, persistence, justified anger, heat, and unfathomable beauty. She is the mother of the land and fiercely protects what she has made. Her body and spirit are connected to the center of the earth, so she always will find another island safe from Na Maka's magic. For now, Pele is happy on Kilauea and can be seen dancing on the mountain every night. Aloha!

CHAPTER 26

BOYNTON CANYON

oynton Canyon in Sedona, Arizona, is an exceptional goddess site whose sacred history and exquisite physics have few rivals. The canyon is the home of Kamalopukwia, Old Lady White Stone, the grandmother spirit of Boynton Canyon. She is the keeper of knowledge of the medicine plants and animals of the Southwest. Kamalopukwia was one of the first People to emerge from the inner Earth after the Great Flood, according to Yavapai spiritual history.[1]

The red rock canyonlands of Sedona have been considered sacred since prehistoric times. Pilgrimages were made to these holy lands from as far south as Central America and as far north as Canada, for good reason. Sedona is one of the most condensed and diverse anomaly sites in the United States.

The canyonlands were considered so sacred that no one lived there until the Spaniards appeared in the 1500s. The canyons were used only for medicine and spiritual knowledge, ritual and ceremony. When Native American medicine men and women gathered herbs or animal talismans they sought out the most powerful medicine plants and animals available. These, of course, came from the sacred centers of power, one of which is now called Boynton Canyon.

Photo by Bernyce Barlow

Rock formations at Boynton Canyon near Sedona, Arizona watch over the medicine plants and animals of this sacred source.

There are many sacred canyons in the area. Boynton's popularity as a primary electromagnetic vortex draws thousands of people each year. Its influence is said to affect approximately ten square miles. With so many anomalies in the area it is a hard call, but I have seen a line of demarcation, along Dry Creek Road, that clearly shows a change in plant life outside the influence of Boynton's energy field.

If you have known the spirit of place of Boynton for a long time, she will teach you things about herself and Gaia. If your exposure to Grandmother is a short one, she will teach you things about yourself. Emotions become amplified in Boynton. Ecstacy states are second nature here, so be prepared.

In my research, some of the most bizarre incidents in which I have been involved happened in Boynton Canyon or the Sedona area. Being somewhat of a skeptic, I had dismissed as hysteria many of the second-hand and some of the first-hand stories people told me. Boynton Canyon changed my mind.

If there were not even a trickle of energy in Boynton its beauty would suffice as a trigger for inspiration. Salmon-, orange-, and amber-streaked rock formations stretch across the high desert floor like enchanted castles or holy cathedrals. Light is caught up in the circadian rhythms of the canyon, and colors come and go like spirits.

The largest concentration of flora species in Arizona exists just a few miles away from Boynton. On a one-and-a-half-mile stretch of the Oak Creek Trail there are 136 species of wild flowers. Much of this collection has found its way into the canyonland network, adding contrast and softness to the stark, startling beauty of the surrounding rock formations.

Pine, cactus, sage, and manzanita mingle with oak, willow, and sycamore along a temperamental creek. In season, the aroma of sweet wildflowers competes with the spice wind of the desert, a true goddess scent that awakens balance.

As a goddess site, Boynton Canyon is a powerful reminder of all aspects of womanhood and its challenges. The intense energy fields amplify the lessons of Kamalopukwia, those of medicine and spiritual depth, lessons about time dimensions and psychic imprint, dreaming and the meaning behind the dream symbology. Grandmother addresses these things to the goddess nature in us all and shakes it up in Boynton Canyon, hoping it will settle somewhere as good medicine.

Blessings will come to the good women and men who have met the spirit of place of Boynton Canyon face to face, for they have seen themselves through the eyes of nature, a magnificent reflection of Gaia in all of her glory and splendor.

Photo by Doug Deutscher

Medicine plants from Boynton Canyon were considered more powerful than those found outside the canyonland network. Yellow flower pollens for ritual paints were also collected in Boynton.

CHAPTER 27

GIANT SPRINGS

It is most interesting how the spirit of place can influence the development of an area. Along the banks of the Missouri river near Great Falls, Montana, is a goddess site called Giant Springs. This is one of the largest fresh water springs in the nation, pumping out 7.9 million gallons of water per hour. The water stays a cool 54 degrees and has been carbon dated to be about 3,000 years old.[1]

When the Lewis and Clark expedition arrived at Great Falls, Montana, on June 18th, 1805, Captain Meriwether Lewis wrote in his journal, "The largest fountain I ever saw and doubt if it is not the largest in America."[2] There is no doubt that these springs truly impressed the explorers as well as the Plains Indians who had recognized the spirit of place of the springs for hundreds of years.

Visually, the springs stand out as the Missouri river rolls past their place of emergence. Green plants and mosses rest just below the shallow surface, giving the springs an underground garden effect that is most delightful. As it bubbles to the surface, the spring water releases its energy; at 7.9 million gallons per hour there is a lot of energy to be released. More often than not, large springs like these automatically create mini-electrical vortexes that energize and rejuvenate the mind, body, and spirit.

Aside from the immediate effects of Giant Springs, there is another more subtle change brought about by the spirit of place of the site. That influence is what has made Giant Springs more than just a tourist attraction. It is a place where the personality of the land has gently pushed developers to create an atmosphere within which the spirit of the springs can work to bring about positive and protective change.

Years ago, the Native Americans realized the springs acted as a nursery to the smaller fish of the Missouri. The temperature of the water was just right for them and since the springs flowed from the banks of the river a natural barrier was created that allowed the fingerlings to grow up. The springs nurtured the children of the Missouri River, which rolled quietly by, as if on tiptoe, so that it would not disturb the babies. Years later, a man-made hatchery was built at Giant Springs, no doubt influenced by the spirit of place at the site.

The hatchery was finally built, pleasing the spirit of place of Giant Springs. With so much exploitation of the Missouri's fish population, the hatchery had its work cut out, but in partnership with the springs the project was successful. Today, about 1.3 million fish are raised and distributed each year within a 150-mile radius of Giant Springs. Using the springs' consistently temperate waters, Kokanee Salmon

Photo by Bernyce Barlow

Giant Springs at Great Falls, Montana, inspired the Lewis & Clark expedition. This photo shows the springs merging with the Missouri River, making this a powerful goddess site.

and various strains of trout are nurtured in the twenty-four outdoor raceways, forty interior troughs, and ten incubators. The only fish health biologist in the state of Montana is stationed at Giant Springs. He watches over the hatchlings with a paternal eye. Disease and parasite investigations, brood-stock testing, fish kill investigations, and technical health evaluations are all a part of his job. Those who work at Giant Springs know they are in partnership with the spirit of place of the site and take their work very seriously. Giant Springs is a perfect example of what benefits can occur when this type of partnership is formed.

Giant Springs is a goddess site whose function was not only recognized but expanded upon, noting that even a spirit of place like Giant Springs needs a little help now and then. The Missouri river has more to contend with now such as pollution, dams created to generate electricity, and controlled runoffs. Her children must deal with these obstacles as well, which sometimes leaves them dead in the water. What the springs could once accomplish by themselves has been overwhelmed by man's intervention in controlling and regulating the Missouri. The fountain's spirit of place had to exert a great deal of influence to inspire the government to build the hatchery in order to continue the cycle of life that was once protected there.

If you find yourself in this area, plan to spend some time with the mother spirit of the Missouri river at Giant Springs, for there is more to the site than the springs and hatchery. There are waterfalls to sit beside and rocks to climb, trees to sit beneath, and islands (no longer used by the grizzly bears) to explore, just as Lewis and Clark did. The original landscape of Giant Springs is gone, making way for 218 acres of park that surrounds the springs, hatchery, and visitor's center, but the ambiance is much the same as it was when first recorded by Meriwether Lewis. The springs will revitalize you and bring to the surface the nurturing instincts of the land, just as they bring to the surface the goddess waters that flow freely beneath the earth.

CHAPTER 28

THE LAVENDERIA OF THE LUISENO

In the early 1700s the Luiseno tribe was well established in what is now called the San Luis Rey Valley, just inland from Oceanside, California. The Luisenos had been preceded by the Shoshone tribe by a thousand years, and archaeological finds at burial and tool sites suggest the valley has been inhabited for at least ten thousand years. The valley itself was first described by the explorer Fray Juan in 1769 as "large and beautiful, so green that it must be planted." Indeed, the valley was a Garden of Eden, with fresh springs that collected in a natural basin, and wonderful weather. The valley was close to the sea with all its resources, yet inland just enough to provide abundant game for its population. Along with the discovery of the San Luis Rey Valley came the first historic accounts of its inhabitants, the Luisenos.

When the Spanish arrived in Southern California, the Luisenos lived in communities at either end of the fresh water basin. Their houses were similar to those of their neighbors, made of reeds, palms, or grass tied to a dome or conical wooden framework. When the huts got too dirty they burned them down and in a short time built others.

Clothing was optional and appeared to be more for celebration and adornment than for practical use. The men wore capes of bear and elk with skirts of net and feathers. The nets, made from the fiber of the agave plant, were also used for fishing. During religious and political rites the men painted their bodies with abstract patterns and colors. The women of the tribe dressed themselves in aprons made from small skins and adorned themselves with shells and seeds found in the area.[1]

The religious hierarchy of the tribe was similar to the other coastal bands in California. There were several classes, among them the political leaders and their shamans. Like the Chumash, the Luisenos were somewhat superstitious and adamantly believed that if they as a people ignored the *Chingichngich*, the political/religious leaders of the tribe, a disaster-like disease would surely follow. This belief allowed the Chingichngich to keep a tight rein on the loyal Luiseno population, whose fear of spells and witchcraft was strong.

Strep and staphylococcal infections were common among the coastal tribes, as was tuberculosis and valley fever (which surfaced again after the California Northridge earthquake of 1994). Occasionally, people died of contaminated water and food, or hunting and hiking accidents. The average life span was about twenty-five or thirty years; a forty-year-old was almost unheard of.

Despite some of the obstacles the Luisenos faced, their lives were satisfying. The valley life was pleasant, there was little concern for personal property other than clothes, shelter, adornment, and food. The ocean not only provided sustenance, but sports and cool weather when it got too hot inland. The lowland was full of springs and rivers with wild grapes and berries for the taking. The Luisenos developed a method for leaching out the bitter acids from the acorns in the region to make a sweet flour for tasty breads and other foods, a process their predecessors had not yet stumbled across. When the missionaries arrived to settle in the valley it had been tamed.

Photo by Bernyce Barlow

The Mission of San Luis Rey is located a few miles inland from the ocean, in the Valley of San Luis Rey.

Around 1798, Mission San Luis Rey was built, under the direction of Fray Antonio Peyri.[2]

By all accounts, Fray Peyri was a very loving and giving father to the Luisenos, but when the secularization of the mission occurred in the 1830s the protection and tutorial role of Mission San Luis Rey changed dramatically. Indian land grants were not recognized by the Mexican government and girls from the village were used for sex and as slaves of government officials. The original intent of Fray Peyri, much to his remorse, became a farce as the internal structure of Mission San Luis Rey began to fall apart. By 1844, there were no more than 400 Luisenos in the valley, by 1860 there were 108, and ten years later the census could account for only twenty-five. The mission grounds fell into scattered ruins and not until the late 1890s was restoration even considered.

Sections of Mission San Luis Rey have been carefully restored, but none are as delightful as the Lavenderia in the southern garden area. The archaeological restoration of this section was done between 1955 and the early 1960s. The Lavenderia was originally a series of fountains and pools used for bathing, drinking, laundry, and gardens. There was an arched adobe gateway with a turnstile, to keep out livestock, followed by a long brick staircase. On either side of the staircase, artistic stone spouts captured for drinking the spring water flowing from the side of the hill. The water ran through charcoal-filtered aqueducts ingeniously built by the Luiseno. The stairs led to a plaza with decorated bathing pools and laundry basins. Since the water ran continuously it was always fresh. Beyond the pools and basins were the gardens where beans, melons, vegetables, and an orchard were planted.

Photo by Bernyce Barlow

A stone gargoyle once channeled spring water into the Lavenderia.

Photo by Bernyce Barlow

Water from a separate acequia flowed through a charcoal filter, which purified it for drinking. Note the lime kilns in the upper right corner of the photo.

The restoration of Mission San Luis Rey and the Lavenderia is ongoing. Since the completion of its last restoration in the 1950s, the Lavenderia is again in need of work. Fortunately, the task is a pleasant one because the environment of the garden is so congenial. The gargoyles, aqueducts, and bathing pools of the Luiseno are very much a part of the living chronicle that the tribe left behind before disappearing into history. May the Lavenderia always be with us as a testament to the lost people of the San Luis Rey Valley, its history, and its charm.

THE WARRIOR

CHAPTER 29

WARRIOR SITES

A warrior site is established according to its physics, holy history, and psychic imprint. These are places of power that stir the primal instincts for survival. This is not to say that women do not have these instincts—they do, but the instincts for provision and survival lie close to the surface within the male psyche and are easier to tap into. Feminine instincts for survival run deeper and are not as accessible. This does not mean that when you visit a warrior site you will begin to beat your chest and chase game. It simply means that an acute awareness takes over that keenly sharpens one's senses.

The energy at warrior sites characteristically is electric or morphogenic. These energy patterns emit upward and can administer a real charge. Morphogenic fields are known to promote dreaming, so it comes as no surprise that many hunting-increase sites like Grimes Point, Nevada, were picked as ceremonial centers.

It is also important to study the holy history of a site to understand the psychic imprint it may impart (for better or worse). The Waha'ula heiau, near the Kalapana entrance to Volcanoes National Park on Hawaii, is a fine place to study psychic imprint. The high-walled temple was built in the thirteenth century by Pa'ao, chief priest to the ruling *ali'i*, and it was dedicated to the most blood-thirsty of all the gods, Ku.[1]

Thousands were sacrificed at this temple whose god boasted to be the "divider of lands." The psychic imprint left here has been etched into the face of the ruin and can be clearly recognized given a little time.

There are other sites whose imprint is not so distressing—warrior centers whose imprints are most inviting. In Southern California's

Photo by Bernyce Barlow

This monzogranite white tank formation at Barker Dam consists of a horizontal and two vertical lift joints. Joints are small fissures that cut rock by pressure, expansion, or the release of stress.

Joshua Tree National Monument there is an area called the Wonderland of Rocks. It is an incredible maze of massive monzogranite boulders that covers about twelve square miles.[2] The Wonderland is under the influence of the Pinto Mountain fault, and demonstrates a tremendous amount of energy. The boulders' crystalline composition makes them frequency conductors, boosting the energetic wave patterns indigenous to the area like monolithic antenna.[3]

The *neuro* effects at Joshua Tree are quite noticeable, especially near a spot called Indian Cove at the northern edge of the Wonderland. The tribes who lived in this area often frequented the Wonderland to hunt Big Horn sheep, a primary staple of desert bands. This is evident from the rock paintings left on the sides of the colossal boulders by hunting expeditions that recorded animals, hunters, weapons, and symbols for increase. Rock art is found in a number of places throughout the monument site. In Joshua Tree the presence of rock art usually marks a sacred site, so keep a sharp eye out for any petroglyphs you may find. Be careful not to touch the art as oil from your hands can discolor it or cause it to fade. The psychic imprints found at Joshua Tree are usually quite endearing.

Another type of warrior site that carries the male ambiance are the dreaming caves of the Chumash Indians of California. There are literally dozens of caves tucked away along the coastline of Southern California from Malibu to San Louis Obispo that were used for the spiritual purpose of dreaming and visions. Not all the caves are along the coast; some are located further inland but the rock art depicted on the walls in the caves tells of a particular kind of journey, the kind one takes while experiencing an altered or dream state.

To understand the spirit of place within the dream caves, it helps to know a little bit about the Chumash religious structure. The Chumash society was divided into social classes: the usual chieftain aristocracy, and a class of prestigious canoe captains, the craftsmen, the laborers, and several kinds of shamans that specialized in certain functions. These medicine men or shamans served in specific capacities that aided the tribe. There was the shaman of weather, the swordfish shaman who controlled the fishing bounty and influenced the sea. There was a healing shaman who sucked illness from a person and sent the poison to the enemies of the tribe, and a bear shaman who turned into a bear, the symbol of fierce power that protected the Chumash. Although the duties of the shamans differed, they did share one thing in common, the dreaming caves.[4]

Only the men could qualify as shamans in the Chumash society. Their power was associated with their ability to see visions and dream answers to problems facing both individuals and the tribe. These visions and dream answers were induced by a drink called *toloache* in Spanish. It is a hallucinogenic derived from the sacred, but deadly, *Datura meteloides* better known as Jimson Weed. This practice was widespread throughout the West and Southwest among a variety of tribes. Once the toloache took effect the shamans would retire to the dreaming caves.[5] They sometimes recorded their dreams on the walls of the caves during an altered state. What we see today are the drug-induced records of visions and dreams that guided the shamans of the Chumash.[6] As you can imagine, the psychic imprint found within the caves is indelible!

The strength of a warrior site can be found in its intensity, no matter if it is a hunting increase site, a dreaming cave, or a war god heiau. This intensity can be felt in the air, in the ground, and in the spirit. It benefits all of us to examine our personal awareness of the survival instincts that we possess. By utilizing the energies found at many of the warrior sites we can do just that. These sites have the uncanny ability to hone our instincts into tools for survival that we can integrate into our daily lives, even in the big city. Keeping that in mind, let us further examine some other warrior sites whose energies are quite powerful and unique.

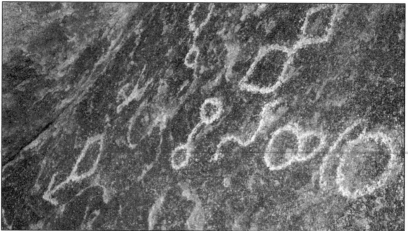

Photo by Bernyce Barlow

Petroglyphs at the Barker Dam area in Joshua Tree National Forest were left by the Serrano and Chemehuevi tribes who inscribed their most sacred symbols onto the monzogranite boulders and cave walls of the area.

CHAPTER 30

PU'UKOHOLA HEIAU: HILL OF THE WHALE

P u'ukohola is a warrior site. The history, imprint, and purpose of the site has created a spirit of place that is undeniably masculine. Pu'ukohola means "Hill of the Whale" and it was here that Kamehameha built the temple that made him king. To understand more about the spirit of place at Pu'ukohola it helps to know its holy history.

Kamehameha was having a tough time conquering the island of Hawaii because his cousin and arch rival, Keoua, had a strong following in the southern region. Kamehameha needed a stronger army to defeat Keoua so he sailed off to conquer Maui, Lanai, and Molakai. While on Molakai, Kamehameha got word Keoua was on the attack in the northern region of Hawaii, Kamehameha's home.

At wit's end, Kamehameha turned to the great prophet Kapoukahi for guidance. He sent his aunt to the island of Molokai to the prophet's temple. There Kapoukahi considered Kamehameha's plight and responded with a prophecy that sparked a wildfire in the young king's heart. Kapoukahi promised that Kamehameha would eventually conquer all of the Hawaiian islands if he followed to the letter the prophet's advice.

Photo by Bernyce Barlow

Hawaiian altar at the base of the Hill of the Whale, where islanders often leave fresh fruit, flowers, and feathers. The shark heiau is a short walk from this spot.

Kamehameha was told to build an elaborate temple in honor of Ku, the family war god. The temple was to be built on the knoll called Pu'ukohola, near the village of Kawaihae on the island of Hawaii. It was to be built exactly to Kapoukahi's specifications. Prescribed ceremonies and sacrifices had to be performed right on schedule. To omit, change, or miss any ritual, or to conduct it at the wrong time would thwart the outcome of the prophecy.

In 1790, the construction of the temple began. Kamehameha put all his time and energy into making sure the building of the temple was done properly. His enemies took advantage of the distraction and banded together to attack the temple while it was under construction. They felt if they could disrupt even one ritual, the prophecy would not come to pass. Kamehameha and his kahuna pules did not miss a beat. They brutally drove the invaders back into the sea and completed the temple in the summer of 1791.[1]

Upon completion, Kamehameha invited his cousin to the temple dedication. Why Keoua came remains a mystery. Perhaps he resolved to put his fate in the hands of the gods. Whatever the reason, he came on his own accord, and was killed immediately before he stepped on shore. Keoua's death was the last of the rituals prescribed by Kapoukahi. He was to be the primary sacrifice at the dedication of the

Photo by Berryce Barlow

The prophecies of Kapoukahi came true upon the completion of this temple located on the Hill of the Whale.

temple. His death was the signal for Kamehameha to begin his campaign to conquer all of the islands.

In 1794, Kamehameha reclaimed Maui, Lanai, and Molokai with a vengeance. In 1795, Oahu was conquered. By agreement Kauai joined the Hawaiian empire in 1819. The death of Keoua had ended any opposition on the Big Island, so by 1820 the prophecy of Kapoukahi had been fulfilled.

This kind of history leaves an impression or imprint on the spirit of place at a site. The Hill of the Whale is a fine example of this. There is also an energy wellspring that emits from the base of the knoll. Obviously, Kapoukahi knew about this wellspring and felt its characteristics would give the young king the edge he needed.

Today, the temple is delicate at best. It is *kapu* (forbidden) to venture farther than the dirt road below the heiau. Earthquakes, use, even truck traffic from nearby Highway 270, have all played a part in shaking up the structure so Hawaiians have asked that the temple be admired but not explored. This does not mean you cannot benefit from the physics of the site, nor does it mean the spirit of place of Pu'ukohola is not accessible. It most certainly is.

There are several other smaller temples in the area including the shark heiau (which gives me the "willies") down by the bay. Since Pu'ukohola is kapu, park your vehicle at Spencer Beach or the information center above the temple and walk to the temple's base. I would also suggest a stroll down to the bay or some quiet time on the knolls that stretch to the beach. It will give the spirit of place a chance to stir up the warrior side of your spirit. What better place for this to happen than at Pu'ukohola?

CHAPTER 31

MO'OKINI LUAKINI

On the northern end of the island of Hawaii stands the Mo'okini Luakini Heiau. The temple sits on a knoll that overlooks the Pacific ocean and the sky. There are no coconut trees or sandy shores surrounding the point where the temple is located; well-kept grounds and the heiau are the only things to be found there. This helps to keep the focus on the site.

Mo'okini was built under the watchful eye of Kahuna Kuamo'o Mo'okini around A.D. 480. The construction of the temple was an act of faith and determination. The basalt stones from which the temple was built were said to come from as far away as the Polulu Valley, fourteen miles away in the Kohala Mountains. Along a human chain consisting of 15,000 to 18,000 men, the stones were passed one by one, from sunset to sunrise. With the rising of the sun, the temple that had been built in less than a day was dedicated to the war god Ku.[1]

The dimensions of the temple were an important part of its construction. It was built in the shape of a parallelogram, with slight variations here and there. The temple is thirteen feet wide at the top and fifteen feet wide at the bottom. It stands around thirty feet high. Each of the four walls varies in length. The southern wall is 112 feet long while the northern wall is 135 feet in length. Similarly, the west wall measures 267 feet long, while the east wall is 250 feet in length. Mo'okini is one

Photo by Bernyce Barlow

The temple (heiau) at Mo'okini, dedicated to the war god Ku, was built in less than twenty-four hours, from one sunset to sunrise.

of the island's largest temples, and the fact this massive stone structure was built in such a short period of time adds to its mystique.

Within the enclosure of the temple was the *luakini,* a sacrifice house made of wood or stone, a temple within a temple. At the entrance to the luakini was a *lele,* or stone altar. The inner temple was the sacred place of the priests from which Hawaiian magic was conducted, usually from a wicker hut within the luakini called an *anu.* Passing from the inner enclosure to the outer enclosure there is a small room located at the door of the outer entrance. This room is where the humans being sacrificed were killed, often by clubbing, before putting their bodies on the lele.[2]

The ruling chiefs, the *ali'i nui,* came to Mo'okini to fast, pray, and hold ceremonies honoring the gods. Many human sacrifices were made at the temple to appease Ku and lesser deities. Although the blood of sacrifice no longer seeps onto the stones of the altar at Mo'okini, a lei, a quarter, or a bottle of rum might be found instead, reminding us that the Hawaiian culture runs like deep water that can surface at any time.

I have mixed feelings about this site. I have been drawn to it like a moth to a fire a number of times. Once, on a Good Friday, I nearly rolled a rental car trying to get to the temple by noon. There had been seasonal rains and the dirt road leading to Mo'okini is not always maintained. Deep depressions in the road were full of tropical rainwater and the banks were slippery and wet, yet a driving force inside of me compelled me to do what I normally tell others not to do. I was determined to get to the site or I would roll the car trying. There was no time to hike it, I had to be there by noon, and I was reduced to tears. Oh, I got through all right (I drive a Jeep at home), but the desire to be at that site at a certain time was overwhelming me to the point of my being foolhardy—and that wasn't the first time this site had such a draw on me.

Photo by Bernyce Barlow

Mo'okini sacrifice altar in the inner temple was often used to appease the angry gods, or to gain their favors.

I made the self-imposed deadline before 12:00 noon and settled into the site. There was no one else at the temple (nobody crazy enough to drive in).The day was beautiful and crystal clear as I wandered among the stones inside the temple walls. When I came across what appeared to be an altar I glanced at my watch—it was noon. Suddenly, I became aware of all the lives that had been lost to Ku. It was a heavy feeling as though my body was very tired, coupled with an underlying feeling of resignation that was most disturbing. It was as if the psychic imprints of the lives sacrificed at Mo'okini were rebelling against the spirit of place. Then a rumbling sounded from the sky overhead, almost inaudible over the crashing of the waves, but I heard it and looked to the heavens. The burden was gone. I had never experienced an ecstacy state quite like this before, and in a way I hope I never will again. I continue to go to Mo'okini, but not without reservation. Each time I recall the Good Friday incident a bit of sadness creeps in. No other heiau in the islands draws me the way Mo'okini does, like a moth to the fire.

Over the past 1,500 years, members of the Mo'okini family have served as guardians or *Kahu* of the temple and continue to do so. In 1963, the Mo'okini Luakini was recognized as a National Historic Landmark. In 1978, Mo'okini was presented to the state as a bicentennial gift from Castle and Cooke, Ltd., and the trustees of the Bishop Estate of Hawaii. The current Kahuna Nui of the site is Leimomi Mo'okini Lum, a direct descendant of high priest Kuamo'o Mo'okini.

CHAPTER 32

ULM PISCUM

Fifteen miles outside of Great Falls, Montana, traveling east toward the Sun River, is a high plateau called Ulm Piscum. Typically a piscum is a mesa or plateau with straight up-and-down cliffs. The Native American tribes would stampede the buffalo over these cliffs by placing their fastest warriors, disguised as buffalo, in front of the herd—buffalo have very poor eyesight. Then the hunters at the rear of the herd would cause enough commotion to start the stampede. The herd followed the disguised braves over the cliffs. The braves leading the stampede escaped being trampled by tucking themselves into ledges dug into the cliff walls before the stampede. To assure a quick kill, small, deep penetration arrowheads were shot directly in the buffalo's heart. The kill itself was sacred, making the piscum a sacred site.[1]

Although there were many piscum sites throughout Montana, Ulm was the location of the Summer Circle. The Summer Circle was a gathering of friendly tribes that came together to share in ceremonies, barter, and the hard work of the buffalo kill. Obsidian from Idaho was traded for fur and meat. Sioux horses were traded for Utah salt and Canadian tribes brought the bounty of the high country to exchange for goods from the Great Plains. Hard work and celebration during the Summer Circle assured safe passage through the ravages of the cold winters.

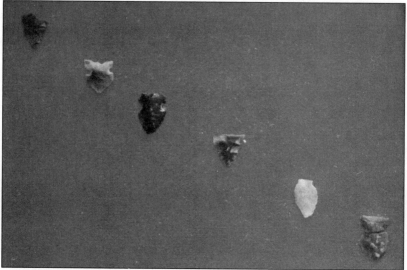

Photo by Bernyce Barlow

Small penetration arrowheads used to kill buffalo that had been driven over the edge of the mesa. The arrowheads were made to penetrate the heart for a quick, merciful kill.

Remnants of blackened firepits and rutted circles made by thousands of teepees over many hundreds of years are still visible etched into the hard cover of the plains of Ulm. At the base of the cliffs layers of buffalo bones lay exposed as a reminder of their sacrifice. Today, rattlesnakes and a prairie dog town keep watch over the piscum. There are rattlesnakes in great numbers at the base of the site, forcing the visitor to walk softly among the buffalo remains.

The spirit of place at Ulm is finely tuned to the cycles of life and death. The instinct for survival is very strong here and charges the will to survive and provide. The ceremonies that left such a psychic imprint on the site demonstrated an understanding of the delicate interaction between nature and man. If you stand on the edge of the piscum and look down on the remains of the Summer Circle you can clearly feel the raw electric energy of the site.

Ulm is a warrior site, a primal plateau whose holy history and ambiance was created and chosen by the warriors of the plains. It is a site that should be approached with understanding and respect. In doing so, the story of Ulm will unfold, giving you a glimpse backward into a time when sacrifice was both celebrated and mourned, a time owned by the warrior.

CHAPTER 33

THE CALIFORNIA INTAGLIOS

iant ground figures are found throughout Baja, Arizona, California, and Nevada. These figures represent human, animal, and ritual symbols belonging to the ancient tribes. The figures can be as large as 300 feet in length and are called *intaglios,* an Italian term used to describe an engraving technique.

The figures are divided into two categories, rock alignments and gravel effigies. Rock alignments were made of rocks embedded or stomped into the ground, while gravel effigies were made by raking the topsoil away from the outline, leaving a figure or symbol. The desert pavement was the palette for both types of ground pictures.

Desert pavement was created by erosion through wind and water. As the topsoil of the basin was carried away, loose pebbles settled and compacted to create a natural tile floor. It was into this pavement that tribal artists pounded or scraped rock pictures. After the figures were created the erosion continued. The heavier picture rocks settled into the desert pavement and left us with the intaglios of North America.

Although there are many intaglios (especially in the Panamint Valley of the lower Colorado drainage basin), the Blyth Intaglios are the most renowned. The largest figure in the group is 171 feet long. These ground pictures are spread out over two mesas in three locations looking across the Colorado River. To fully appreciate these works of art an

Photo by Bernyce Barlow

This intaglio may represent Mastambo, the creator, according to desert culture. His two helpers were mountain lions.

air trip over the area helps put them into perspective, but a close-up look at these figures shows off the pavement palette.

The Mohave and Quechan tribes say the human figures are effigies of Mastambo, the creator of all life, and the animal figures represent Hatakulya, the mountain lion/person who helped the creator. The Blyth Intaglios grouping was a sacred site where Mastambo was worshiped through dance, ceremony, and prayer. Because this was a ritual site, very few artifacts have been discovered there, making chronological research difficult at best. Attempts to date the intaglios have fallen short; the construction of the Blyth intaglios took place somewhere between 500 and 2,000 years ago.

There are an estimated 100 intaglios sites in the West. Death Valley, Red Rock Canyon in Kern County, Wildrose Canyon in Inyo County, Yuha Wash, and the Chocolate mountains in Imperial County all host alignments and effigies as well as cairns and circles.[1]

Ground circles and cairns are sometimes found near or incorporated into the intaglios, especially at rock alignments. The ground circles range from three to seven feet in diameter and were made by leaving the original gravel base, removing the larger rocks from the formation, then pounding the fine gravel into a tightly packed circle. The circles in Death Valley are said to be dreaming circles still used by the local tribes.

A typical cairn might look like a pile of rocks five feet in diameter and two feet high polished by a glaze called desert varnish. A cairn may be the foci of an alignment or set off to the side. There may be many cairns grouped together like those found in Inyo County (eighteen cairns at one site), or a single cairn tucked away on some obscure mesa. At some intaglios sites, ground circles and cairns are found in combination. Unfortunately, the original purpose of these shrines has been lost.

The Hopi tribe of Arizona say one of the giant ground pictures found at Blyth is a deity belonging to their Fire Clan. This figure was made when the Fire Clan and Water Clan quarreled at this tie. Legend

Photo by Berryce Barlow

This Blyth intaglio has been claimed by the Hopis of Arizona. They say it is the representation of their fire clan deity. Hopi clan markings have been found nearby, lending credibility to their claim.

says the figure is barring the Water clan from returning to this area by reading the deity's outstretched arms. To give credibility to this story, Hopi clan migrational signatures can be found nearby, along the cliffs of the Colorado River. A picture of the Fire Clan deity (looking very much like Mastambo) and the story of the clan quarrel has been recorded by the tribe.

I have found a great similarity between Great Basin petroglyphs and the symbolic intaglios. The Desert Culture was one of nomadic migration and the idea of people traveling from north to south is not at all foreign. Just the fact that the ground pictures were made over a span of at least a couple of thousand years gives credibility to the theory that interpretation of this ancient form of symbology may be found to the north and northeast, the migrational seats of the Desert Culture.

Also in question is the purpose of the effigies. Because there are two styles of intaglios, representational and abstract, it is difficult to know what the effigies represent. Representational intaglios like the figure of Mastambo at Blyth are easily understood because the figure clearly represents a human. Abstract intaglios are more difficult to interpret because they use a symbology that is no longer understood. Hunting, fertility, rain, and creation appear to be the subjects at some of the sites, but this is only speculation. Some intaglios are much older than others and were already in place when migrating tribes found and integrated them into their culture, adding their own flavor to the lore of the intaglios.

We may never unlock all the mysteries of the intaglios but we can strive to protect them so our children can perhaps answer the questions we could not. Until then, the intaglios will continue to perfect themselves by using the forces of nature to set in stone the unique beauty and character of an ancient form of praise and worship.

CHAPTER 34

THE TEMPLE MOUNDS OF MEXICO

The early explorers who set sail for the Americas called the land the New World. Imagine their surprise when they found a highly organized old world civilization committed to a strict political and religious system already established upon their arrival. As far back as the Olmec occupation of Mexico, before 1200 B.C., there had been taxes to pay and deities to appease by the indigenous peoples of Mezoamerica. Part of the cultural backbone of these peoples was the building and use of magnificent pyramid-type structures. By the time the explorers arrived centuries later, in the early 1500s, the last great pyramid-building civilization, the Aztecs, was on the decline.

Unlike Egyptian pyramids that were used as energy-enhanced tombs, the pyramids of the New World were used as ceremonial platforms. Actually, they are not really pyramids at all, but four-sided, flat-topped polyhedrons. The pyramids of Egypt have four triangular sides that meet at a point on top. The architectural differences between the pyramids of the New World and Egypt are clearly significant. Archaeologists prefer to call the polyhedrons temple or platform mounds but most people still refer to structures like the Pyramids of the Sun and Moon, near Mexico City, as pyramids.

A typical temple mound layout consisted of one or more mounds grouped around a ceremonial plaza. The mounds, built in successive

Photo by Bernyce Barlow

Avenue of the Dead, the main thoroughfare of Teotihuacan. By 450 B.C. this city covered eight square miles and had a population around 150,000, although its radius of influence took in the entire central plateau.

steps, were faced with cut stone blocks and generally had a stairway carved into one or more of the sides. The substructure was often made of rubble, limestone, or earth, although mortared blocks of stone were also used. The outer surfaces of the temple mounds were quite lavish, decorated with bright colors, stucco moldings, carved lintels, and statues. The interiors were usually very cramped, with a few narrow windows for ventilation.[1]

One of the oldest temple mounds can be found in La Venta in southeastern Mexico. It is an Olmec site dating back to 1200 B.C., long before the Inca, Mayan, Toltec, or Aztec civilizations had been established. These great empires carried on the traditions of building temple mounds in the Olmec style centuries after the Olmec's demise. There are literally hundreds of temple mounds scattered throughout the Americas. Three of the largest mounds are the Pyramid of Choluta, outside of Puebla, Mexico, the Pyramid of the Sun, near Mexico City, and Huaca del Sol in Moche, Peru. Other grand temples such as Tikal, Copan, Palenque, Uxmal, Mayapan, Uaxacyun, and Chichen Itza can be found from Guatemala to the Yucatan peninsula, and up through Central Mexico.[2]

The widespread locations of these ceremonial temples suggest a highly structured political and religious system throughout Mexico. We know from codices from as far back as the sixth century that the religious systems of the Mayans, Toltecs, and Aztecs incorporated human sacrifice into their rituals. When Cortez first came across the Pyramid of the Sun he saw thousands of Aztec warriors lined up to sacrifice themselves during a major ceremony. To give one's life in battle or as an offering was the highest honor a warrior could hope for. After Cortez and his Catholic soldiers got over the shock of witnessing the ritual sacrifice they began to recognize similarities between the Aztec religious structure and their own.

The Catholics of the 1500s believed Dante's image of heaven, hell, and purgatory was fairly accurate. When they learned that the spiritual significance of the construction of the temples followed the same principles of Dante's Mountain of Purgatory, they were amazed. Clearly, the temples had been built in successive steps representing thirteen heavens, their deities, nine hells, and an omnipotent God whose symbol was a cross. There was even a god/man, Quetzalcoatl, born of a virgin, resurrected after death, and who was a patron of the priests.[3] Without any understanding of global myth, the Spanish concluded that earlier Catholic contact had been made, perhaps by St.Thomas, hence the similarities. As a matter of fact, Cortez was at first mistaken for Quetzaloatl by the great ruler Montezuma and given free run of the city. The mistaken identity gave Cortez time to undermine the Aztec chief and eventually cause his death.

Photo by Bernyce Barlow

The Pyramid of the Sun was begun around 100 B.C. and continued to be transformed until A.D 750.

Photo by Bernyce Barlow

Aztec God figure found in the coastal jungle of Mexico.

Actually, Quetzaloatl was borrowed by the Aztecs from the Toltecs. His history goes back to the tenth century—or longer if you allow for Mayan influence. He was originally a god of the soil. The Aztecs elevated him to a position that represented life and death. He was a god of vision who foretold that he would return as a fair-skinned, bearded man in a certain year. When Montezuma saw Cortez he truly believed he was meeting Quetzaloatl.

The recorded history of Mexico began with the building of the temple mounds. There are still many mounds to be uncovered but as more are discovered the missing pieces of the pyramid puzzle can be put together. The gods and their duties, holy days, and religious rituals, as well as daily life, were all depicted on the temples and throughout the plazas that surrounded them. As we become more familiar with these mystical temples, a rich and colorful culture comes to life, a culture that is part of the cornerstone of the New World.

CHAPTER 35

MOUNT SAN ANTONIO

The story of Mount San Antonio, affectionately referred to as Mount Baldy, is about to unfold. The mountain has always represented the struggle between the land and water, but as time went on the people of Southern California forgot about the spirit of place on Baldy and turned the mountain into their backyard playground, without a clear comprehension of its destiny or background.

The San Gabriel mountain range where Mount Baldy reigns has always been a haven from the blistering summers that affect the Los Angeles Basin. The Serrano and Gabrieleno tribes called Mount Baldy their home in the hottest season, then migrated toward lower elevations and warmer weather when the snows came. The Gabrielenos left us the first hint of the mountain's struggle through an epic describing its origin.

The story tells of the creation of the human race and of Mount San Antonio. Together the Landgod and Seagod had planned to make humans but they could not agree where the eyes of the humans should be placed. The Landgod wanted two eyes in the front of the head but the Seagod wanted one eye in the front and the other in the back. The two of them could not come to an agreement so no decision was made. The Seagod went away for a day to think about where the eyes of the human should go, but when he returned he found the Landgod had gone ahead and made the humans without his approval.

Photo by Bernyce Barlow

Mount San Antonio, locally known as Mount Baldy, is a refuge for Angelenos during the hot summer months and a winter playground when the snow falls.

Seagod was furious. He opened up heaven's rains and released the underground springs and rivers in order to raise the oceans to sweep away and drown the humans. Landgod, in order to save the humans, raised up the earth and made mountains for the humans to stand on safely above the water. Mount San Antonio was the highest of all the peaks, the mountain that the humans and Landgod stood upon in the wake of the flood of Seagod's rage.[1]

The myth is more than just charming, it is a story that establishes the personality of the spirit of place on the mountain. The struggle against the hex of the Seagod is nothing new to the mountain. The last hundred years of its development clearly show that this battle rages on and sooner or later someone is going to win!

In Southern California captured water is essential to survival. In the late 1800s when the Ranchos and missions began to establish themselves in the region, water was diverted from mountain rivers and springs for crop irrigation and for daily living needs. The details of water agreements (who got how much and when) were usually peacefully made among those who built, maintained, and used the irrigation ditches. On Baldy, however, water disputes broke out all over, and alliances were formed and protected with "Smith and Wesson" law. The mountain was in turmoil for a number of years, until the San Antonio

Water Company was founded in the early 1900s. This company was followed by a number of others who merged and split and sold out to others to become what it is today, a conglomerate of three hydro-electric plants and dams that supply the valley below with enough electricity to light up the basin. The threat of this captured water is very real to Baldy in every sense of the word and the mountain "knows" it.

Mount Baldy was formed by tectonic movement. It is an extremely steep mountain whose surface naturally sheds a great deal of sediment. The high erosion rate of Mount Baldy was balanced in the past by an alluvial fan that spread the sediment out into the valley below. Where there was once lush vegetation to help this process along, now there is concrete to hurry the overflow to the ocean. This process has been impeded by modern developments. Instead of the well-balanced alluvial fan, housing tracts and roads channel the runoff quickly before it has a chance to percolate into the ground, lowering an already inadequate water table. In the meantime, behind the dams technology tries to remove the tons of sediment shed by Baldy but is losing the battle. The base of the mountain is encased in its own sluff and probably sooner than later is going to have to shake it off or be poisoned. As loyal as Landgod has been to humankind on Baldy, must he die for them?

The San Andreas faultline sits precariously close to Mount Baldy. Its thrust was what formed the mountain, with the help of seismic systems like the San Gabriel and San Antonio faults. The ground is already shaking. Are the dams on Mount Baldy going to hold? Maybe, maybe not! Seagod has not forgotten the fight, neither has Landgod. The human's eyes were placed in the front of the head so they could live on the land. If they cannot successfully do this, perhaps Seagod was right and one eye should have been in the front and the other in the back.

I know Mount Baldy very well and have watched the disposition of the land dramatically change. There have always been tiffs on the mountain like the time in 1887 when 400 miners were working the gold veins at once, using powerful hydraulic pipes with three-inch nozzles to chisel the mountain away with turbo-boosted water. Under the hydraulic pressure the red clay of the mountain's hillsides washed off and poisoned the watersheds and irrigation systems in the valley below. The San Antonio Water Company had to step into the picture and restrict the mining to half an hour at a time to allow the runoff to settle. The restriction made mining unprofitable, forcing the companies to look elsewhere.[2]

Then there was the glorious 1928 resort called Camp Baldy, developed by the Curry family of Yosemite resort fame. The resort was really a mountain city with swimming pools, more than seventy-five cabins, dining rooms, an amusement park, and a casino with a 7,000-foot dance pavilion that extended over the streambed. Camp Baldy was chic, the happening place to be, until a flood in 1938 destroyed the place. The Currys did not rebuild, moving to Idylwild on Mount San Jacinto instead to build yet another resort.

There have often been Landgod/Seagod tiffs on Baldy's turf such as the ones described above that have casually affected its spirit of place, but the mood of the mountain these days is not to be taken lightly. It doesn't appear to be getting ready for the usual tiff but for another full-scale battle with Seagod. Mount San Antonio seems destined to play out this story for as long as it stands. The feeling is uncomfortable.

In the very near future those who have settled snugly into the valleys at the foot of Mount Baldy may receive a wake-up call. They are already living on the crest of an alluvial fan and a floodplain that needs at least three dams to keep it above water. The once-unconstrained landscape of Mount San Antonio has been changed enough to affect the entire ecosystem of the mountain. Natural history has shown that the mountain's homeostasis system is intact and well and able to rebel, so consider yourself warned.

Until the battle breaks out again Mount Baldy will provide high ground for those who respectfully seek refuge from the basin below. The pines, willow, and sycamore of the mountain slopes will continue to give shade from the summer sun, the rivers will run clear, the hot springs will bubble and pool, and the canyons and waterfalls will continue to provide a place for each other.

Mount Baldy is a powerful mountain. In 1995, a number of people met their deaths there. Treacherous avalanches confronted snowboarders and skiers who refused to stay in designated areas, cars careened off cliffs, and hikers were swallowed up by steep, snowy slopes. The mood of Baldy should not be toyed with these days; it is ill and has become intolerant and angry. It is a mountain that should be approached with respect and an understanding that the forces of land and water are active and escalating. Do not get caught up in the battle; it belongs to the spirit of place!

Sacred Mountains
Sacred Trees

CHAPTER 36

SACRED MOUNTAINS

S ome mountains are sacred, and have been recognized as such down through the ages. Peaks like Mount McKinley, Mount Rainier, the Matterhorn, Mount Ararat, Mount Fuji, Mount Sinai, and Mount Kilimanjaro are sacred mountains whose history and names are familiar to us. You can tell that a mountain is sacred by the way it speaks to you at the base of its waterfalls, at its summits, or as you walk through its forests looking for meadows and wildflowers. A sacred mountain has a history that goes as far back as the mountain itself, an undeniable history of faith and physics that will not be beaten down by neoteric science.

In Arizona, the San Francisco mountains tower above the high desert plateau. They are the home of the Hopi *kachinas*. These peaks have been the sacred mountains of the Hopi tribe since their last emergence near its base. Every winter the kachinas come down from the mountains and visit the Hopi, staying until midsummer when they return to the coolness of the forests. Kachinas are not gods. According to Hopi legend they originally came from another world far out in space. The kachinas have always been with the Hopi, helping them from emergence to emergence like messengers.[1] During a ceremonial kachina dance, the wearer of the kachina mask takes on the spirit of the kachina, allowing the spirit to manifest itself in the flesh. The kachinas govern the elements like rain and wind so they are very important in sustaining the life of the tribe. The San Francisco mountains are equally important to the Hopi, being the home of these powerful spirits.

Across the ocean on the Hawaiian island of Maui stands another sacred mountain called Haleakala, The House of the Sun. Thirty-six thousand feet high from ocean floor to mountain top, this Hawaiian holy site rises 10,000 feet above the aquamarine Pacific and dominates the central part of the island.[2] Ascending Haleakala, lush green slopes, tropical gardens, and eucalyptus groves greet you as only paradise can. As you go higher you will see the personality of the mountain change, revealing the more serious side of its nature. The verdant scenery switches to a desolate moonscape in a heartbeat and the tropical serenity of the coast gives way to the nervous emptiness of the barren crater at the mountaintop.

Haleakala is a dormant volcano which has not erupted for about 200 years. Pele used to live there until her sister chased her out. The mother of Maui, the trickster god of the Hawaiians, lived there as well. Legend says she complained to Maui that the days on the mountain were too short to dry her freshly washed bark cloth. The sun simply passed by too quickly, so Maui set out to snare the sun over the mountain to slow down its pace so his mother's clothes could dry. By doing this Maui pleased both his mother and the other islanders who enjoyed the long summer days, that thanks to Maui had now come to the island.

The Iao Valley in the West Maui Mountains is another Hawaiian sacred site. It was considered a sanctuary for the *ali'i nui* and their priests. There is a stone there called the Needle that protrudes from a volcanic base. Its shape is phallic, and it was considered a warrior site by the male islanders. Many rituals and ceremonies were performed at the base of the Needle and within the Iao valley itself. It was the sacred site of kings.[3]

One of the West's most sacred mountains is Mount Zion in Utah. Its significance belongs more to this age than perhaps any other. If wisdom was something tangible it would look like Mount Zion. Approaching the mountain is like approaching a holy elder. Its spirit of place is strong and powerful. The pile of bills lying by the telephone doesn't seem important in the presence of the patriarch. On Zion, a ubiquitous character prevails, molding the human daily struggle into a cosmic lesson of nature. The holy alcoves and stone chapels chiseled into the

Photo by Deb Olson

The Iao Valley (Valley of the Flesh), in the West Maui Mountains is the burial site of the Hawaiian kings. The bones of kings were hidden here to keep their manna (energy) from being using against their families. This Warrior site, with its obvious phallic symbolism, is kapu to women. A rock outcropping on the peak bears a remarkable likeness to President Kennedy.

mountain by wind and water provide sanctuary for the pilgrim who comes here to worship. Any attitude other than holiness is inappropriate on this most sacred of mountains.

The Cascades stretch from Northern California to Canada and encompass many sacred peaks that stand out like snow-capped jewels dangling from a volcanic chain. Mount Lassen, Mount Shasta, Mount Jefferson, Mount Hood, Mount St. Helens, Mount Baker, Mount Adams, Mount Shuksan, and Mount Rainier are all considered sacred by the Native American tribes that live near them. Although these mountains are brothers, sisters, aunts, and uncles of each other they demonstrate a fierce independence that can be seen in the intrinsic spirit of place at each site.

It is unfortunate that these beautiful mountains have to fight for their lives from time to time—not from the lightning fires or droughts that occasionally make an appearance in any given area, but from over-lumbering and over-mining the soil.[4] We are building even more ski resorts and more condos on the slopes of these sacred sites, not only stripping them of their flesh, but of their dignity as well. Finally, there seems to come a time, as we saw with Mount St. Helens, when enough is enough and the sacred mountains reclaim what is rightfully theirs, at our expense.

Unlike the Cascades whose sacred mountains were shaped individually by volcanic activity, the High Sierras of California (and a small part of Western Nevada, near Tahoe) were not. The High Sierras were created by a thrust of the earth tilting upward and east, causing a single block of rock to emerge. Technically, the Sierras are one big sacred mountain.

The High Sierras are known for their extremes. Not only is the tallest mountain in the continental United States, Mount Whitney, found there, but in the wilderness of King's Canyon National Park is the nation's deepest canyon (from rim to floor). Parks in Yosemite, Sequoia, and Tahoe display this exceptional beauty daily in an earth show that is simply called Sierra Nature. When you combine extreme conditions and a person with an extreme personality there is no limit to what may happen. The late environmentalist John Muir loved the Sierras. He would climb to the tops of the tallest trees during violent storms and hang on for dear life as he was blown and tossed by high winds and torrential rain.[5] It was his way of understanding the earth forces on a profound level. It comes as no surprise to those who know the extreme spirit of place of the Sierras that Muir chose them as his home base.

Photo by Bernyce Barlow

The High Sierras, above Lake Crowley display their nature in the extreme. The famous naturalist John Muir loved this part of the Sierras and spent much of his time here.

Not all mountains and ranges have the reputations of those mentioned above. There are a few places of power that demonstrate a sinister side to their personality. Mount Diablo near Clayton, California is one of those mountains. The earlier tribes of the area used to say the mountain was a bad medicine site that should be avoided. Being the curious person that I am, I found myself renting a cabin for a week on the slopes of Mount Diablo to explore the possibilities of the peak. It did not take long for me to find out the legends were based on truth.

The power of suggestion is an undeniable force. We see it work in medicine, spirituality, and self-empowerment all the time. Because of this, I tried to keep an open mind during my research as to the character of the spirit of place on Diablo, but no matter how I tried I felt uncomfortable on the mountain. One evening during the middle of the week I decided to confront my feelings about the mountain and pigeonhole them into compartments labeled superstition and suggestion. After doing this I fell asleep feeling sure the next day would prove to be more productive and less emotional. Was I ever wrong!

The next morning I woke up to a pitch-black environment. At first, I thought it was the middle of the night and was going to roll over and finish my sleep when I saw a slender ray of sunlight coming through a crack in the wall by my bed. If it was morning, why was it so dark in the cabin? As I got up to investigate, a crunching beneath my feet was the first indication something was wrong. There was a musty scent all around me that had not been there the night before. To my horror, when I turned on the light I saw millions of flies in layers several inches thick covering the walls, windows, and floor of the cabin. My stomach turned, the hair on my arms went haywire, and I freaked. I had come to the mountain to experience its spirit of place. Been there, done that, I was gone. It was my last visit to Diablo. The tribes were right—it was a bad medicine mountain.

Fortunately, most sacred sites do not display such a diabolic atmosphere, although it is important to understand that such places do exist. For the most part, sacred mountains are places of healing and wisdom where we can come to discover and interpret that which is mysterious to us. The answers to our deepest questions are acted out every day in a passionate power play along the peaks and hollows of the sacred mountains. To come to these mountains with an open mind and a spirit of appreciation will allow the ambiance of mountain to teach you the secrets that it has found out through time and place. If you seek answers then find the places where Gaia manifests the gift of teaching, the sacred mountains, the holy mountains of wisdom whose peaks tap on heaven's door and whose feet are firmly planted in the good earth.

CHAPTER 37

ELDEN PUEBLO

At the base of Mount Elden in Flagstaff, Arizona, is a site that began to flourish between A.D. 1100 and 1250, under Sinagua influence. The Hopi recognize the site as *Pasiwvi*, the ancestral home of many of their clans. Today, Elden Pueblo is a model of public monuments that inspire local communities to educate themselves and others about their regional history.

Research and excavation has always been considered the private domain of scientists and expert laymen. Sites are fenced off from the public and little information is released until the teams are ready to publish their finds. Sometimes this takes years, even decades—consider the Dead Sea Scrolls. At Elden Pueblo the public has been invited to be a part of the excavation team, opening the doors wide for new theories, idea exchanges, and enhanced appreciation for local Native American history and culture.

Elementary students and college students alike find themselves side by side brushing away centuries of earth deposits that cover the pueblo. The public digs are well organized and educational, supervised by the Coconino National Forest archaeology team and supported by various organizations. Local housewives, blue- and white-collar employees, retired seniors, as well as visitors to the Flagstaff area are all encouraged

Photo by Bernyce Barlow

Excavations at Elden Pueblo are open for public participation. Cooperative programs finance, supervise, and excavate the site. This pile of rubble is now a restored site containing more than seventy rooms.

to participate. This public approach has transformed a pile of rubble and stone into what is quickly developing into a fully excavated and in some instances restored site for future generations to enjoy.

The pueblo itself is located in a Ponderosa pine forest at the base of what is now called Mount Elden. A spring near the ruins was no doubt the main water source for the community, always a contributing factor in the settlement of a village. The Ponderosa forest provided abundant game and ample food staples to the residents of the area. To the near northeast and south varied elevations (environmental zones) expanded the variety of medicine plants, food, fur, and meat available to the community.

Elden pueblo has some unique characteristics that add charm and intrigue to the site. Just outside the main pueblo complex are three burial sites, cemeteries actually, holding the remains of the west's ancestors. Outside the complex are activity areas with roasting pits and storage bins plastered into the ground. At first glance one might think the plastered pits are latter-day additions to the park, but archaeologists tell us these pits were part of an activity area that included a good old-fashioned barbecue!

The pueblo was built from stones from Mount Elden. It has approximately sixty to seventy rooms. There is a large community room with a built-in bench where residents met for a myriad of reasons. Slab-lined ventilator shafts within the rock walls provided fresh air to the

Photo by Bernyce Barlow

Photo by Bernyce Barlow

Stone walls (bottom photo) emerged as the Elden Pueblo site was excavated. The top photo was taken during the early stages of excavation.

rooms throughout the pueblo. These shafts are seen throughout the Southwest in pueblo architecture. As work continues on the pueblo, more clues will be revealed for us to ask questions about, find answers to, or just wonder about.

What is known so far is that Elden was a trade and craft community. The Wupatki complex to the north and the Walnut Canyon community to the near southeast were probably involved in trade with the Elden residents, as well as those clans and bands living in the Via Verde Valley or those on the Mogollon Ridge. The Elden community was diverse, and farmed the alluvial fan near the pueblo, expanding their trade and consumption products. This, combined with their ability as hunters, gatherers, clan craftsmen, not to mention their reputation as a spiritual center (Hopi), gives Elden a unique personality.

Enhancing the personality of the pueblo is the imagination of those who are involved in its excavation. The pueblo is a working program that dispels the myth that the treasures and enlightenment of the past should remain in the hands of a few. This is especially apparent while listening to people discussing the ruins during a public dig. Then Elden comes alive, enchanted, as legends of the Hopi Snake and Badger clans are told beneath the whisper of wind blowing through the Ponderosa. The diggers discuss the influence of the Sinagua on the Hopi culture over a peanut butter and jelly sandwich, they wash down lunch and new-found ideas with a cool drink, then continue their field work energized as much by the fellowship as the food. It is a wonderful experience to share!

Perhaps in the future more ruins will be opened to the public for organized education and excavation. Not all sites are appropriate for this kind of public program, but those that are should be candidates for similar programs. A hands-on approach to the cultural history of our continent has time and time again engendered a compassionate understanding, accompanied with a respect that can only come from applied knowledge. Elden Pueblo demonstrates this as a working principle that brings ideas, people, and the past together.

CHAPTER 38

THE SACRED SPRUCE

The Blue Spruce forests of Colorado and New Mexico have inspired artists like D. H. Lawrence and Carlos Nakai to produce works of music and literature that have been recognized worldwide. These spruce forests are sacred to many tribes of distinction including the Hopi, Tiwa, and Ute. The color of the spruce tree dominates the landscape. It is a color that resonates deep through the soul, drawing the observer into herself or himself. The Hopi say that the spruce tree has magnetic properties that draw the clouds that bring rain. Interestingly enough, they understand this as a principle of physics that modern technology has not yet figured out!

At the spectacular ruins of Mesa Verde, Colorado, there is a large spruce, approximately 200 years old, whose story has been handed down from generation to generation in the Southwest. It is the story of Salavi (Spruce), the leader of the Black Badger clan of the Hopi. Many of the clans had settled at Salapa, the Mesa Verde complex, and were apparently quarreling among themselves; then the crops failed and the springs dried up, leaving the area inhabitable. It was time to migrate to the south in search of harmony and provisions. Salavi sternly warned his people their discord might have caused the problems they were facing and not to repeat their mistakes at the next settlement.

Photo by Bernyce Barlow

In the Sangre de Cristo Mountains, this birch boundary marker is found in a blue spruce forest. Just beyond the marker is an eagle nesting grounds sacred to the Tiwa tribe.

Salavi was very old and could not make the trip with his people, but he instructed them to return in four years and search for a sign that his spirit was with them. He further added that if the misfortune of the clans had anything to do with him there would be no sign.[1] Four years later the elders of the tribe returned as Salavi instructed. The spring that had dried up was gushing water, and beside it grew a young spruce tree that was four years old. The Hopi believe that Salavi's spirit had been transformed into the spruce as a sign of his faithfulness and righteousness. Pilgrimages are still made to Mesa Verde to the spruce tree called Salavi by the Hopi.

CHAPTER 39

THE ALBINO REDWOOD

The coast redwood (*Sequoia sempervirens*) grows along the Pacific coastal region from Southern Oregon to Central California. It is a cousin of the giant sequoia and the dawn redwood of China. These three cousins are the last of their genera on the planet and are found in extremely restricted regions. Careless exploitation has reduced the coast redwood to less than four per cent of its original population, an example of what can happen to a species when willful neglect replaces environmental respect.

The redwoods are said to be the tallest trees on the earth (their only rival is the Australian eucalyptus), reaching heights of nearly 400 feet, with diameters as large as twenty-five feet. Their average age is 2,500 years old. To experience a redwood grove is truly humbling. You cannot help but feel as if you are standing within a living cathedral among the redwoods.

A redwood tree can yield a ton or two of timber, and after cutting, given forty years, will reproduce offshoots suitable for another round of lumbering. High amounts of tannin in the redwoods' trunks protect the trees from insect infestation and bacterial decay, making the species very popular with the lumber industry.[1]

Photo by S. Veirs

Albino Redwood branches. Note the white needles. This tree grows in a public area at Fernwood Campground in Big Sur.

Redwood branches are close together, supporting flat needle-like leaves indicative of its family trait (Cypress). The flat needles retain moisture from the humid coastal environment, providing the massive amount of water it takes to keep these giants alive. The needles have a dark blue-green hue, giving the forest a feeling of density and darkness, even in the brightest of sunlight.

Occasionally, a saprophytic redwood sprouts from a grove, commonly referred to as an albino redwood because its needles are silver-white instead of green. This redwood cannot manufacture food by photosynthesis. Instead, it derives its nutrients from organic matter through its root system by utilizing a unique enzyme found in all saprophytic plants. Some of the most common saprophytes include certain types of mushrooms, bacteria, molds, and fungi. The Indian Pipe plant is saprophytic, as are many species of the white orchid genus *Corallorhiza*.

At one time the coast redwoods of the western Pacific were abundant. Their sheer mass was overwhelming, but out of millions of trees there were only a few albino redwoods. That is why the Native Americans of the region considered them sacred and set them aside as holy trees.

Today only a handful of these albino trees can be found in the redwood forests. The Big Sur area of Central California hosts a few and others can be found scattered here and there up the coast. All of the albino redwoods living today are in the process of dying out. They are among a group of offshoots from mother grove trees that have fallen or have more likely been cut. With no source for photosynthesis, these youngsters will also die in just a few years.

The Esalen Indian tribe of Central California disappeared around 450 years ago, leaving very little behind in the way of history. Pieces of the Esalen puzzle can be gathered here and there from some nearby tribes in the Carmel Valley, but 450 years is a long time to preserve a small pocket of culture that was assimilated by an exacting mission system. (See Chapter 17 for more information about Esalen.)

It is known, however, that the albino redwood was somehow connected with the burial rituals of the tribe. They referred to it as the "ghost tree." When researching the locations of albino redwoods no longer standing, burial grounds are usually found within a quarter of a mile from the tree. Burial beneath mounds of dirt was the common practice of the central coastal tribes and if there was an albino redwood in the area it somehow became incorporated into the burial ceremony.

There is also an enchanting legend of a young Indian maiden named Monacca and her experience with an albino redwood. Apparently, Monacca became lost in the dense redwood forest after dark while picking spring berries for her grandmother. After trying in vain to find her way through the pitch-black forest, she remembered a story told around the campfires of the elders about the albino redwood.

It was said on a moonlit night the "ghost tree" danced with moonbeams and its glow could be seen from the heavens. So, Monacca decided that if the sacred tree could be seen from the heavens then surely it could be seen from the ridge directly above her. The sacred tree was near Monnaca's home and she could use its glow, like a dagger of light, to guide her safely through the forest.

Monacca climbed up to the highest point on the ridge. Since there was a full moon, once she got above the tree line she could see much better. There, far in the distance, was the albino redwood shimmering silver-white like a candle in the dark. She followed the illuminated giant until she could see the flicker of the watch fires of her camp.

Once Monacca was safely tucked into her bed she dreamed of the sacred tree and how it had saved her life. While she was sleeping, the spirit of place of the redwood forest taught her a special melody that was the wind tune of the "ghost tree." In her dreams Monacca saw the tree from the heavens and soared on the wings of her imagination through its snow white branches. It was a night she would never forget.[2]

This legend is the only story that can be connected to the Esalen and the albino redwood. It is as if the albino is destined to follow the Esalen down the path of extinction.

It is possible for other albino trees to sprout, but not probable. The surviving trees along the coast are literally numbered. Even with a life span of a couple of thousand years they are running out of time. So, if for no other reason than homage, the albino redwood will remain a noble symbol for sacred trees and sacred people.

CHAPTER 40

THE PAINTED DESERT AND THE PETRIFIED FOREST

O n the high plateau of northeastern Arizona is the Painted Desert. The region is known for its contoured, multi-hued mountains that appear to change color throughout the day. The soft layers of desert stone are molded by wind, rain, and erosion. Although the elements of the desert are harsh, they help to carve personality into the gullies and chasms of the mountains, creating the exposed layers, shapes, and brilliance of the Painted Desert.

From a distance the Painted Desert is inspiring. Overlooks such as Chinde Point, Tawa Point, and Tiponi Point are scattered up and down Interstate 40, but within the interior of this region are some wonderful sites that you might miss if you just view the landscape from a lookout point. The Black Forest area can be reached by a four-mile loop trail in the Painted Desert. The trail will take you to a forest of trees, petrified by natural processes.

The Painted Desert extends along the Little Colorado river from the Grand Canyon to the Petrified Forest National Park. With the main body of the Petrified Forest just next door to the Painted Desert, most

Photo by Bernyce Barlow

In the Painted Desert of Arizona are fossils dating 225 million years old. Dinosaurs once roamed freely here when the desert was a fertile marshland.

visitors include it in their itinerary. Between the Painted Desert and the Petrified Forest there is quite a lot to explore. Other than Black Forest there are four other main concentrations of petrified trees: at Blue Mesa, Jasper Forest, Crystal Forest, and Rainbow Forest.

At one time the sequoia tree, a cousin to the Coast Redwood, grew in abundance in this region. Fossil remains of the sequoia from the Jurassic Period have been found here, as well as fossils of other coniferous trees that are between 180 million and 135 million years old. Some fossils date back even further—around 225 million years. What are now the carved stone mountains of the Painted Desert and the Petrified Forest used to be a marshland that supported an ecosystem of giant forests where dinosaurs roamed.

A chain of natural processes killed the forests, leaving timber lying around like pick-up sticks. The area is also volcanic, with high amounts of silica found in the sediment and water. As streams, rivers, and floods carried the logs downstream, they collected in areas that eventually became buried under hundreds of feet of volcanic ash and sediment. Silica permeated the trees which were soaking in the silica-laced water table, turning the wood to stone and creating the petrified forests we view today.[1]

There are other points of interest in this region. Petroglyphs and a solstice calendar can be explored at the Anasazi ruins of Puerco. On one of the walls is a figure of a man holding a coyote by the tail. The Hopi call this a *poko*, an animal that does things for you. Newspaper rock, a delightful collection of Native American petroglyphs, can be viewed from an overlook off a short side road just south of the Puerco River. Agate Bridge, a fallen log that spans a forty-foot ravine, is also a popular attraction, as is the Rainbow Forest Museum.

No matter where you go in this region, you are sure to find sites and exhibits that display the changing earth. There is mystery in this desert. A long-range view of the area shows an effective display of nuance, but the real color of the region is found up close in its history. Minerals like iron oxide have stained the silica, creating rainbows in the petrified wood, and crystals of various shades and content are found in the canyons and on the summits of the stone mountains. When the sun illuminates these colors they become as gemstones buried in a desert painted by nature herself.

It is hard to imagine that this barren landscape was once a swampy marshland. What was left is a curious assortment of puzzle pieces that have allowed us to put together the big picture. Although it once looked nothing like it does today, the Painted Desert has recorded the brush strokes of prehistory, giving us a glimpse into the colorful archives of the West set into a petrified stone gallery of delight!

CHAPTER 41

EARTH'S ELDERS: THE BRISTLECONE FOREST

Eٮast of the Sierra Nevada, within the boundaries of the Inyo National Forest, lies the White Mountain range. The world's oldest living trees, the Bristlecone pine, are found here. For over 4,000 years these trees have managed to survive on the barren alkaline slopes of White Mountain, at elevations over 10,000 feet above sea level. At this altitude the ultraviolet light is intense, but the trees appear to thrive on it. With a forty-five-day growing period and little water, the Bristlecones have adapted their development accordingly. Some trees grow as slowly as one inch (in girth) every hundred years. It appears that this slow growth cycle contributes to the longevity of the tree.[1]

The Bristlecone pines (*Pinus longaeva*) originate from a highly resinous and shaggy pinecone that grows from the tips of the branches on the tree. The pine needles on younger trees come in bundles of five that densely cover the branches. The trees that take root on the moister slopes of the range grow more quickly, with wider girths and more height, but they do not attain the longevity of the trees that grow in the more inhospitable areas. As you might imagine, the wood of the Bristle-

Photo courtesy of USDA, Inyo National Forest

Ancient Bristlecone trees in the Inyo County National Forest live for thousands of years. These trees are found only in the White Mountain range of central California.

cone pine is extremely dense; the older the tree the denser the wood, and the denser the wood, the more resin is produced to keep the tree alive. This highly concentrated resin keeps the wood from rotting or succumbing to disease.

After the wood on the Bristlecone has developed for thirty to forty centuries, the growth pattern begins to die out. The abundance of youthful needles disappear and the supple branches harden to snags. Life on the tree is reduced to a few needle bundles growing from a thin ribbon of bark after the wood is dead. Because of the nature of the Bristlecone, as long as there is any sign of life on it anywhere it is considered living, even if it is only a few needles here and there. As the trees naturally die out, the elements begin to shape the wood through erosion, wearing them down slowly, layer after layer in the reverse process of their growth. Ice and ruthless winds carve, sculpt, and polish the timber into ancient pieces of art that look gnarled and ghostly when set against the arid backdrop of the surrounding peaks. A thousand years after their official death, these trees continue to hold on to the earth through sheer tenacity, still a part of the haunting landscape.

The spirit of place of the Bristlecone Forest is obvious when you come face to face with these, the oldest living trees on the planet. The forest has an emotional impact on people almost immediately. These most ancient trees impart the wisdom we so often seek out among our elders. The forest evokes respect and empathy for the nature of time. As a human whose life expectancy on earth is relatively short in comparison to the Bristlecone tree, time is put into perspective; it becomes distinctly precious.

Life is not easy, not for the Bristlecone tree nor for humans. In our youth there is strength and vibrancy, we bend and grow. In old age we become eroded by forces that are inevitable, but we hold on through determination and perseverance until the very end. The Bristlecone tree does not perish under the same conditions that a human would, but, on the other hand, humans have adapted to adverse conditions much in the same way the Bristlecone has. Steady growth builds strength and character, whereas growing too fast can cause weakness

Photo courtesy of USDA, Inyo National Forest

The Bristlecone pine tree weathered by extreme conditions, grows approximately one inch in 100 years.

in any structure, shortening its lifespan. It is harder to erode a strengthened form, be it a tree or a person. The Bristlecone forest shows us the harshest of conditions can build instead of tear down, given there is enough time (or in the case of humans, patience) allowed for the process to work.

There are many lessons to be learned from the Bristlecone forest. Its spirit of place has been around for a long time. The fact that many of these trees are still living after 4,000 years of facing whatever nature has handed out offers hope for the human race that we too can slow down and adapt. This takes wisdom. The question the forest suggests is: are we wise enough to do that or will we end up like the trees on the wet side of the slopes, tall and fat with relatively short life spans?

If you visit the Bristlecone forest, you will find its spirit of place much like an elder whose parables weave a delightful yarn, full of wisdom and knowledge. Legend lessons are imparted to the visitor that could only be taught by one who is already ancient and wise. It will not take long for you to find this essence, for it is in every tree that has ever grown on the mountain. It can be found in the youth of the seedlings or the hardened wood of the ancients. Even the stumps, dead for a thousand years, echo the consciousness of the forest. A visit to the Ancients will allow that echo to resonate throughout your being, triggering an understanding of a type of time consciousness that spans more than the lifetime of a human or even a Bristlecone tree, a type of understanding that belongs to the elders of our planet. Listen and learn.

OBSERVATION

CHAPTER 42

LITTLE KIDS AND SACRED SITES

One of my favorite roles in life is being Aunt Bernyce. It is a role that brings me a lot of joy and pleasure. With seven nieces and nephews ranging in age from thirteen to newborn, I find myself overwhelmed sometimes with their precious attention. Through the years, I have had the opportunity to watch them discover the world with childlike wonder and awe. Watching them triggers memories of my own first encounters with the earth and helps keep the child in me alive and well. Whatever positive influence I have on my nieces and nephews, their influence on my life is equally important.

Little kids have a way of tuning into things. Watching them follow their natural inclinations often can give us a hint as to the nature of the spirit of place at a site. I quit taking people with little kids to Airport Mesa in Sedona because the electrical energy there makes kids quite active. There isn't much room to run around and I was afraid sooner or later one of them was going to fall off the mesa. Actually, I did not do this for the parents' sake, I did it to be fair to the kids. Settle down or fall down seemed like a setup considering the place throws off such a tremendous upsurge of energy. It was like telling them to keep still at Disneyland or they would get hurt. Since then I have found plenty of other places for kids to run with lots of space and lots of energy. The

Photo by Bernyce Barlow

The joy of discovery, crawdads! The author's nieces experience crawdads, pinchers and all.

nice thing about electrical energy sites is that you can usually keep up with the kids!

Little kids are drawn to the earth. Watch them by a stream or a lake. One of the first things they do is pick up a rock, look at it, maybe throw it; their conscious environment automatically includes their surroundings. As we grow older and get busy we tend to surrender our appreciation for the colorful pebbles under our feet. We take for granted that they are there and walk on without acknowledging them, losing a moment of beauty. Beauty fills the lives of little kids. It can fill ours too, if we take the time to see it as a child would, spontaneously.

I recently found out during a "little kid survey" what they considered a sacred site. Disneyland, the zoo, the beach on a sunny day, somewhere with caves or room to fly a kite, places with dolphins you can touch, and Santa's village were some of the answers given. After a peek at the list, it isn't hard to figure out that little kids are drawn to places where their imaginations can run wild—something to keep in mind next time you are drawn to a sacred site.

Quite frankly, my nieces and nephews couldn't care less about the scientific data of a site. They only care about what the site can do for

Photo by Bernyce Barlow

Shiprock, Navajo sacred mountain, through the eyes of a 10-year-old Navajo child. He has drawn a UFO perched on the upper left edge of the mountaintop, and an alien figure beneath it.

them. That is OK, they are little kids, but they are not too young to be taught to not litter, to be careful with fire, and to respect the nature of the spirit of place where they are. They are not too young to be taught the sacredness life holds and to allow the living to live, or to let those die who must. It is all a part of the circle of life and must be respected. As adults, it is our responsibility to teach the children respect for the earth when they are little kids so they grow up to be big kids who care and later become adults who not only care but can be a part of the solution and not the problem. This kind of education is something we can all participate in actively that will make a difference in the immediate future we are so concerned about.

Little kids and sacred sites go hand in hand. Their innocence allows a spontaneity that leads to adventure. In our search for and research of sacred sites it would behoove us to keep this spontaneity alive within our own spirits. The biblical phrase "be as little children" applies especially well at a sacred site, particularly one to which you are drawn. So next time you find yourself along the banks of a lake or river or walking along a country road, stop for a moment and pick up one of the pebbles under your feet. It will not only give you a moment of discovery, it will help rekindle a delightful feeling of childlike wonder and joy within your soul.

CHAPTER 43

GETTING THERE, BEING THERE

I f you plan on visiting a sacred site, and the key word here is plan, do so with common sense. The planet is a beautiful place, but not necessarily a safe place to explore. The most gentle spirit of place can be treacherous when not given due respect. Occasionally things happen when we travel that we don't plan on, so it helps to be prepared.

It is important that you know your personal limitations when planning a sacred site adventure; some sites are more difficult to get to than others and require a bit of stamina. The great thing about energy centers is there are plenty of them, and many that are easily accessed. If you do hike into a site, make sure you have enough water or purification tablets with you. It is also wise to carry a small first-aid kit in your daypack.

Knowing about the flora and fauna of the region you are visiting is also a good idea. It not only gives you an idea of what to look for but also what to look out for. While I was in Utah I slept on sandbars along the Colorado river. There had been nights that I was so tired from the day's activities I would fall asleep watching the starshow outside my tent. The last night on the river was no exception. I remember feeling little critters I thought to be mice scurry over me, but I was too exhausted to care. As long as they didn't bother me I wouldn't bother them. Imagine my surprise in the morning when I saw a number of cute little scorpions, approximately six to eight inches long, happily darting to and fro around my bedding. Had I been practicing what I preach, I would have been zipped up in my tent tighter than a can of sardines!

Rattlesnakes are also a concern on the trail. Even along paved paths in our national monuments there are snakes and critters to watch out for. Snakes are territorial and will strike if they feel threatened. The second strike is faster and more deadly than the first, so try and stay out of their way if at all possible. If you like to poke around rocks be especially careful.

Knowing the flora of a site is just as important as understanding the fauna. It not only gives you a unique understanding of the medicine plants and ecology of the area; it teaches you what plants can cause you discomfort. Obviously, you would not wear sandals while hiking through a cactus patch, but do you know what poison oak or ivy looks like? Would you recognize a river nettle if you saw one before you touched it? A little bit of awareness goes a long way when it comes to plants; prepare yourself accordingly.

Photo by Berryce Barlow

One hundred-year-old graffiti at the bottom of Montezuma's Well tells us that the ruins were "pot-hunted" long before many of the artifacts at the site could be saved.

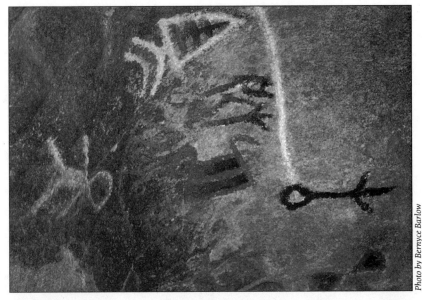

Photo by Bernyce Barlow

This authentic rock art was painted over by a film crew for a movie being filmed in Joshua Tree National Park. The cave where these petroglyphs appear has both a high blowhole and a low hole.

Then there is good old common sense. I burned the hair off my arms when I got too close to a lava flow once. I just had to have that photograph! The incident could have been a lot more serious. It was more of a survival experience than an ecstasy experience, and it really made me think about respecting the power and character at a site.

Visiting a sacred site can be one of the most rewarding trips of your life as long as you come prepared and use common sense. There is a cliché that says "take only photographs, leave only footprints." It is kind of goofy, but it works. There should be an attitude when visiting a sacred site that parallels being in a sanctuary. If you come with the right intentions and stay with an open mind, the possibilities of what you may experience are unlimited. While visiting the sacred centers I hope you find everything you are looking for and more, that the relationship you will find with the planet will be one of depth and emotion, that she will reach out and touch you, enhance you, heal you, and delight you in a way that is just as inspired as Gaia herself. Best of luck and lots of light!

NOTES

Gaia

Chapter 1: Earth Physics

1. Hauck, Dennis William. *National Directory of Haunted Places,* (Viking, New York, 1996).

2. Epton, Sidney and James Loveock. *New Science Magazine,* 1975.

3. Hauck, Dennis William. California Whole Earth Expo, 1995.

4. Father Miguel Mateo. Personal letters to author.

5. Sanders, Pete. *Scientific Vortex Information, An M.I.T. Trained Scientist's Program* (Free Soul Publishing, Sedona, AZ, 1981).

Chapter 2: Air Ions

1. Gamow, G. and John Cleveland. *Physics: Foundations and Frontiers* (Prentice-Hall, Inc., New York, 1960), p. 202.

2. Lyall, Watson. *Beyond Supernature* (Bantam Books, New York, 1988), p. 256.

3. Swan, James. *Sacred Places* (Bear and Co., Santa Fe, NM, 1990), p. 153.

4. Soyka, F. and A. Edmonds. *The Ion Effect* (E. P. Dutton, New York, 1977).

5. Sutphen, Dick. *Unseen Influence* (Pocket Books, New York, 1982), p. 87.

6. Quinn, Jean Ph.D. *Imagine That!* (Jean Quinn, copyright 1995).

7. Sartor, P. "Plateau." *Journal of the Museum of Northern Arizona* (1964).

8. Southwest Parks and Monuments Association. *The Wupatki Trail* (1993).

Chapter 3: Ley Lines and Grid Nets

1. Tilt, David. "Monitoring Ley Energy" (*BSD Journal,* No. 220, June 1988).

2. Cathie, Bruce; B. I. & Temm, P. N. *Harmonic 695,* Reed 1971, and *Harmonic 33,* Reed 1968.

3. Watson, Lyall. *Beyond Supernature* (Bantam Books, New York, 1988), p. 259.

4. Pope, Ilse. "A View of Earth Energies from Continental Europe" (*BSD Journal,* No. 217, September 1987).

Chapter 4: Vortexes

1. Sanders, Pete. *Scientific Vortex Information*, pp. 20, 55.

2. Yavapai tribal history; as told by Chieftess Viola Jimulla before her death in 1966.

3. Barlow, Bernyce; part of an alternative healing program developed by the author while working with abused youth.

Chapter 5: Natural Phenomena

1. *Omni*, Vol. 16 No. 1, October 1993, p. 35.

2. Swan, James. *Sacred Places*, p. 143.

Amplification

Chapter 6: Galleries of Song

1. Watson, Lyall. *Beyond Supernature*, p. 225.

2. Waters, Frank. *Book of the Hopi* (Ballantine Books, New York, 1963), p. 113.

3. Swan. *Sacred Places*, p. 151.

4. Campbell, Joseph. *The Mythic Image* (Princeton University Press, Princeton, NJ, 1974).

5. Collins, Jan. *Shaman's Drum*: Fall 1988, pp. 29–33. An Interview with Burnam Burnam.

6. Nakai, Carlos. *Desert Dance* (Celestial Harmonies, Arizona, 1990).

Mind and Site

Chapter 7: Personalizing the Sacred Sites

1. Jung, Carl. *Higher States of Consciousness* (Eranos Jarhbuck, 1938).

2. Campbell, Joseph. *Myths to Live By* (Bantam Books, New York, 1973), pp. 270–271.

3. Swan. *Sacred Places*, p. 86.

Chapter 8: The Schumann Resonance

1. Lin, Loralee. *Vibrations From Within* (Nordick Press, California, 1990), p. 53.

Chapter 9: Chimayo, The Lourdes of America

1. Mateo, Miguel, S.F., Chimayo priest, personal letter to author, 1994.

2. De Borhegyl, Stephen. *El Santurario de Chimayo* (Ancient City Press, Spanish Colonial Arts Society Inc., Santa Fe, NM, 1956), pp. 2–19.

3. *Sons of the Holy Family: High Road to Taos* (Sons of the Holy Family Press, 1982), p. 9.

Chapter 10: Pu'uhonua O Honaunau

1. Dept. of the Interior (GPO, Washington, D.C., April 1988).

2. His Hawaiian Majesty Kalakaua. *The Legends and Myths of Hawaii* (Mutual Publishing, Honolulu, HA, 1990), p. 46.

Chapter 11: Cataract Canyon

1. *World Wide River Expeditions; Cataract Canyon* (GPO, Washington, D.C., January 1994).

2. *Tag-a-Long Expeditions; Cataract Canyon* (GPO, Washington, D.C., 1994).

Chapter 12: Santa Catalina Island

1. Mallan, Chicki. *Guide to Catalina* (Moon Publications, Chico, CA, 1989), pp. 13, 15.

2. Santa Catalina Island Conservancy. Public domain data, 1994.

3. Wrigley Memorial and Botanical Garden. Public domain data, 1994.

Chapter 13: Oak Creek Canyon

1. Underwood, Jan. *Song in the Night* (Duben and Halbrook Publications, Arizona, 1972), p. 104.

2. Botanical Society of Central Arizona (GPO, Washington, D.C., April 1977).

Chapter 14: The Indian Canyons of Palm Springs

1. Tribal Pamphlet. *Indian Canyons: Palm Springs, CA* (GPO, 1994).

2. Trent, D. *Geology of Joshua Tree National Monument* (California Dept. of Conservation, Sacramento, CA, April 1984), p. 81.

Chapter 15: Mount Shasta

1. Mt. Shasta Information Center. *Mt. Shasta and Shastina* (GPO, Washington, D.C., 1991).

2. Medicine Eagle, Brooke. *Buffalo Woman Comes Singing* (Ballantine Books, New York, 1991), p. 291.

3. *Shasta Caverns* (GPO, Washington, D.C., 1981, Shasta Caverns Inc.).

Chapter 16: The Anasazi Trail

1. Noble, David. *Ancient Ruins of the Southwest*, p. 34.

2. McAuliffe, Kathleen. *Omni,* Vol. 17 No. 5, p. 97. Interview with Linda Schele.

3. Swan, James. *Sacred Places*, p. 57.

Chapter 17: The Sacred Waters of Big Sur

1. Tomkins, Calvin. "New Paradigms." *The New Yorker,* Jan. 5, 1976.

2. Litwak, Leo. "Joy is the Prize." *The New York Times Magazine*, Dec. 31, 1967.

3. Kahn, Alice. *The L. A. Times Magazine,* Dec. 6, 1987. "Esalen at 25."

Chapter 20: Hawaiian Petroglyphs

1. Holmes, Mikelio. *The Case of the Stony Scribbles* (Visitor's Center Publication, 1989).

2. McBride, L. R. *The Petroglyphs of Hawaii* (Petroglyph Press, Hilo, HA, 1969).

Chapter 21: Wupatki

1. *Wupatki/Sunset Crater Volcano* (GPO, Washington, D.C., 1993).

2. The Hopi School, Nevada, 1995: Author's personal files, 1995.

3. Flagstaff Chamber of Commerce: County Printing Office. Public Domain Files, 1995.

4. Wupatki Visitor's Center. GPO, Washington, D.C., 1995.

Goddess

Chapter 22: Goddess Sites

1. Taylor, P. E. *Border Healing Woman* (University of Texas Press, Austin, TX, 1981).

2. Dongo, Tom. *The Mysteries of Sedona* (Hummingbird Press, Arizona, 1988), p. 25.

Chapter 23: Emergence Sites

1. Waters, Frank. *Book of the Hopi*, p. 30.

2. Nixon Library; California, 1994.

3. Rena, Janie. *Tales of the Tiwa*, p. 54.

4. Noble, David. *Ancient Ruins of the Southwest*, p. 162.

5. Swan, James. *Sacred Places,* pp. 226, 229.

6. Waters, Frank. *Book of the Hopi*, p. 43.

Chapter 24: Lunch Creek

1. Sanders, Pete. *Scientific Vortex Information*, p. 48.

Chapter 25: The Kilauea Caldera

1. Bushnell, O. A. (National Park Service, Dept. of the Interior. GPO, 1980).

Chapter 26: Boynton Canyon

1. Sutphen, Dick. *Sedona: Psychic Energy Vortexes* (Valley of the Sun Pub., Malibu, CA), pp. 31–35.

2. Sanders, Pete; *Scientific Vortex Information*, p. 56.

Chapter 27: Giant Springs

1. Montana State Parks and Wildlife Interpretive Association.

2. Great Falls Chamber of Commerce. GPO, Washington, D.C., 1995.

Chapter 28: The Lavenderia of the Luiseno

1. Kelsey, Harry. *Mission San Luis Rey, A Pocket History* (Interdisiplinary Research Inc., California, 1993), pp. 5–7.

2. Sweimler, Joel. *Mission San Luis Rey* (Colour-Picture Publishers, Boston, 1992), pp. 28–31.

3. Weber, Francis. *The King of Missions: A Documentary History of San Luis Rey de Francia* (Weber Press, 1980).

The Warrior

Chapter 29: Warrior Sites

1. National Park Service. *Volcanoes National Park, HA.* GPO, Washington, D.C., 1992.

2. Knapp, Patty. *Walks and Hikes* (M. I. Adventure Publications, Maine, 1989), pp. 7–8.

3. Trent, D. *California Geology* (California Dept. of Conservation, Sacramento, CA, April 1984), p. 79.

4. Anderson, Eugene. *The Chumash Indians of Southern California* (Malki Museum Press, 1989), p. 7.

5. Anderson, Eugene. Bibliography of the Chumash and their Predecessors: *Archaeology Survey Report 61: 1964*, pp. 25–74.

6. *Bureau of American Ethnology. Report 78, 1925*, pp. 550–568.

Chapter 30: Pu'ukohola Heiau: Hill of the Whale

1. Pu'ukohola State Park Service (GPO, Washington, D.C., 1989), "Spencer Beach, HA."

Chapter 31: Mo'okini Luakini

1. *Mo'okini Luakini* (Mo'okini Luakini Inc., Honolulu, HA, 1979. Hawaii State Park Service).

2. His Hawaiian Majesty Kalakaua. *The Legends and Myths of Hawaii*, p. 45.

Chapter 32: Ulm Piscum

1. Montana State Park Service, Ulm Station, 1981.

Chapter 33: The California Intaglios

1. Blyth Chamber of Commerce; Blyth, CA. 1992 information packet, including a 1935 geological thesis survey published by Berkeley Press.

Chapter 34: The Pyramids of Mexico

1. Vasquez, Fernando. *Aztec Temples* (University of Mexico City Press, Mexico City, 1968), pp. 106–111.

2. Romo, Domingo. *Sun and Moon, The Story of Cortez* (Cave Publications, Mexico City, 1965), p. 23.

3. Campbell, Joseph. *Myths to Live By* (Bantam, New York, 1972), p. 7.

Chapter 35: Mount San Antonio

1. USDA Forest Service. Mt. San Antonio Canyon impact report.

2. USDA Forest Service. Mt. Baldy Ranger District, Glendora, CA.

Sacred Mountains and Trees

Chapter 36: Sacred Mountains

1. Waters, Frank. *Book of the Hopi*, p. 202.

2. Dept. of the Interior, Haleakala, GPO, Washington, D.C., 1990.

3. His Majesty Kalakaua. *The Legends and Myths of Hawaii*, pp. 155–173.

4. U.S. Dept. of Agriculture. GPO, Washington, D.C., 1988, p. 17. "Final Environmental Impact Statement."

5. Muir, John. *My First Summer in the Sierras* (Houghton-Mifflin Publishing, New York, 1916).

Chapter 38: The Sacred Spruce

1. Waters, Frank. *Book of the Hopi*, pp. 56–61.

Chapter 39: The Albino Redwood

1. The Redwood Society, Felton, CA. Combined research reports, 1966–1992.

2. Barlow, Bernyce. "Monacca and the Albino Redwood." *1997 Magical Almanac* (Llewellyn Publications, St. Paul, MN, 1995).

Chapter 40: The Painted Desert and the Petrified Forest

1. AAA Tour Book. *Arizona and New Mexico* (AAA Publishing, 1994), p. 57.

2. Waters, Frank. *Book of the Hopi,* p. 128.

Chapter 41: Earth's Elders: The Bristlecone Forest, Ca.

1. *Inyo National Forest Department* (GPO, Washington, D.C., 1994).

BIBLIOGRAPHY

AAA Tour Book. *Arizona and New Mexico.* AAA Publishing, 1994.

Anderson, Eugene. "Bibliography of the Chumash and their Predecessors." *Archaeology Survey Report 61: 1964.*

Anderson, Eugene. *The Chumash Indians of Southern California.* Malki Museum Press, 1989.

Barlow, Bernyce. "Monacca and the Albino Redwood." *1997 Magical Almanac.* St. Paul: Llewellyn Publications, 1995.

Blyth Chamber of Commerce. 1992 information packet, including a 1935 geological thesis survey published by Berkeley Press. Blyth, CA: Blyth Chamber of Commerce, 1992

Bureau of American Ethnology. Report 78, 1925.

Bushnell, O. A. National Park Service, Dept. of the Interior. Washington, D.C.: GPO, 1980.

Campbell, Joseph. *Myths to Live By.* New York: Bantam Books, 19731.

Campbell, Joseph. *The Mythic Image.* Princeton, NJ: Princeton University Press, 1974.

Cathie, Bruce; B. I. & Temm, P. N. *Harmonic 695,* Reed 1971, and *Harmonic 33,* Reed 1968.

Collins, Jan. *Shaman's Drum:* Fall 1988, pp. 29–33. An Interview with Burnam Burnam.

De Borhegyl, Stephen. *El Santurario de Chimayo.* Santa Fe, NM: Ancient City Press, Spanish Colonial Arts Society Inc., 1956.

Dongo, Tom. *The Mysteries of Sedona.* Arizona: Hummingbird Press, 1988.

Epton, Sidney and James Loveock. *New Science Magazine,* 1975.

Gamow, G. and John Cleveland. *Physics: Foundations and Frontiers.* Prentice-Hall, Inc., 1960.

Hawaii State Park Service. *Mo'okini Lauakini.* Hawaii, HA: Mo'okini Luakini Inc., 1979.

Hauck, Dennis William. *National Directory of Haunted Places.* New York: Viking, 1996.

Holmes, Mikelio. *The Case of the Stony Scribbles.* Visitor's Center Publication, 1989.

Jung, Carl. *Higher States of Consciousness.* Eranos Jarhbuck, 1938.

Kahn, Alice. "Esalen at 25." *The L. A. Times Magazine,* Dec. 6, 1987.

Kalakaua, His Hawaiian Majesty. *The Legends and Myths of Hawaii.* Honolulu, HA: Mutual Publishing, 1990.

Kelsey, Harry. *Mission San Luis Rey, A Pocket History.* California: Interdisiplinary Research Inc., 1993.

Knapp, Patty. *Walks and Hikes.* Maine: M. I. Adventure Publications, 1989.

Lin, Loralee. *Vibrations From Within.* California: Nordick Press, 1990.

Litwak, Leo. "Joy is the Prize." *The New York Times Magazine,* Dec. 31, 1967.

Lyall, Watson. *Beyond Supernature.* New York: Bantam Books, 1988.

Mallan, Chicki. *Guide to Catalina.* Chico, CA: Moon Publications, 1989.

McAuliffe, Kathleen. *Omni,* Vol. 17 No. 5, p. 97. Interview with Linda Schele.

McBride, L. R. *The Petroglyphs of Hawaii.* Hilo, HA: Petroglyph Press, 1969.

Medicine Eagle, Brooke. *Buffalo Woman Comes Singing.* New York: Ballantine Books, 1991.

Mt. Shasta Information Center. *Mt. Shasta and Shastina.* Washington, D.C.: GPO, 1991.

Muir, John. *My First Summer in the Sierras.* New York: Houghton Mifflin Publishing, 1916.

Nakai, Carlos. *Desert Dance.* Arizona: Celestial Harmonies, 1990.

National Park Service. *Tag-a-Long Expeditions; Cataract Canyon.* Washington, D.C.: GPO, 1994.

National Park Service. *Volcanoes National Park, HA.* Washington, D.C.: GPO, 1992.

National Park Service. *World Wide River Expeditions; Cataract Canyon.* Washington, D.C.: GPO, January 1994.

Noble, David. *Ancient Ruins of the Southwest.* Flagstaff, AZ: Northland Publishing, 1981.

Omni, Vol. 16 No. 1, October 1993.

Pope, Ilse. "A View of Earth Energies from Continental Europe." *BSD Journal,* No. 217, September 1987.

Pu'ukohola State Park Service. "Spencer Beach, HA." Washington, D.C.: GPO, 1989.

Quinn, Jean Ph.D. *Imagine That!* Jean Quinn, 1995.

The Redwood Society, Felton, CA. Combined research reports, 1966–1992.

Rena, Janie. *Tales of the Tiwa.* Mountain Press, 1989.

Romo, Domingo. *Sun and Moon, The Story of Cortez.* Mexico City: Cave Publications, 1965.

Sanders, Pete. *Scientific Vortex Information, An M.I.T. Trained Scientist's Program.* Sedona, AZ: Free Soul Publishing, 1981.

Sartor, P. "Plateau." *Journal of the Museum of Northern Arizona,* 1964.

Shasta Caverns Inc. *Shasta Caverns.* Washington, D.C.: GPO, 1981.

Sons of the Holy Family:High Road to Taos. Sons of the Holy Family Press, 1982.

Southwest Parks and Monuments Association. *The Wupatki Trail.* 1993.

Soyka, F. and A. Edmonds. *The Ion Effect.* New York: E. P. Dutton, 1977.

Sutphen, Dick. *Sedona; Psychic Energy Vortexes.* Malibu, CA: Valley of the Sun Publishing, 1986.

Sutphen, Dick. *Unseen Influence.* New York: Pocket Books, 1982.

Swan, James. *Sacred Places.* Santa Fe, NM: Bear and Co., 1990.

Sweimler, Joel. *Mission San Luis Rey.* Boston: Colour-Picture Publishers, 1992.

Taylor, P. E. *Border Healing Woman.* Austin, TX: University of Texas Press, 1981.

Tilt, David. "Monitoring Ley Energy." *BSD Journal,* No. 220, June 1988.

Tomkins, Calvin. "New Paradigms." *The New Yorker,* Jan. 5, 1976.

Trent, D. *California Geology.* Sacramento, CA: California Dept. of Conservation, April 1984.

Trent, D. *Geology of Joshua Tree National Monument.* Sacramento, CA: California Dept. of Conservation, April 1984.

Tribal Pamphlet. *Indian Canyons: Palm Springs, CA.* Washington, D.C.: GPO, 1994.

Underwood, Jan. *Song in the Night.* Arizona: Duben and Halbrook Publications, 1972

Waters, Frank. *Book of the Hopi.* New York: Ballantine Books, 1963.

U.S. Dept. of Agriculture. "Final Environmental Impact Statement." Washington, D.C.: GPO, 1988.

Vasquez, Fernando. *Aztec Temples.* Mexico City: University of Mexico City Press, 1968.

Watson, Lyall. *Beyond Supernature.* New York: Bantam Books, 1988.

Weber, Francis. *The King of Missions: A Documentary History of San Luis Rey de Francia.* Weber Press, 1980.

INDEX

Stay in Touch. . .

Llewellyn publishes hundreds of books on your favorite subjects
On the following pages you will find listed some books now available on related subjects. Your local bookstore stocks most of these and will stock new Llewellyn titles as they become available. We urge your patronage.

Order by Phone
Call toll-free within the U.S. and Canada, **1–800–THE MOON**.
In Minnesota call **(612) 291–1970**.
We accept Visa, MasterCard, and American Express.

Order by Mail
Send the full price of your order (MN residents add 7% sales tax) in U.S. funds to:

> **Llewellyn Worldwide**
> **P.O. Box 64383, Dept. K056-6**
> **St. Paul, MN 55164–0383, U.S.A.**

Postage and Handling
- $4.00 for orders $15.00 and under
- $5.00 for orders over $15.00
- No charge for orders over $100.00

We ship UPS in the continental United States. We cannot ship to P.O. boxes. Orders shipped to Alaska, Hawaii, Canada, Mexico, and Puerto Rico will be sent first-class mail.
International orders: Airmail—add freight equal to price of each book to the total price of order, plus $5.00 for each non-book item (audiotapes, etc.). Surface mail—Add $1.00 per item.
Allow 4–6 weeks delivery on all orders. Postage and handling rates subject to change.

Group Discounts
We offer a 20% quantity discount to group leaders or agents. You must order a minimum of 5 copies of the same book to get our special quantity price.

Free Catalog
Get a free copy of our color catalog, *New Worlds of Mind and Spirit*. Subscribe for just $10.00 in the United States and Canada ($20.00 overseas, first class mail). Many bookstores carry *New Worlds*—ask for it!

NORTH STAR ROAD
Shamanism, Witchcraft & the Otherworld Journey
Kenneth Johnson

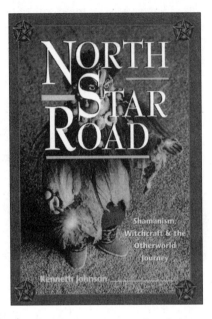

This book reveals—through a compelling mix of scholarly research, global mythology and lucid story-telling—the spiritual roots of Western culture: shamanism.

Shamanism is the most ancient and persistent experience of human spirituality. All European mythology and paganism until the time of the witchcraft trials is based on shamanism. Through an exhaustive study of the trial records and the testimony of the witches themselves, Kenneth Johnson proves that the European peasants accused of witchcraft died, in fact, for the sake of the world's oldest spiritual path.

Shamanism is our universal link. It survives, in one form or another, because the ability to communicate with the Otherworld is integral to the human condition; it is as natural and necessary as sleeping or dreaming. That is why shamanic practice slips through the net of structured theologies, why it survived the Christianization of Europe, and why it's necessary that our culture restore a living contact with the vibrant force of the Otherworld.

North Star Road also includes exercises that give you a feeling of the kinds of techniques used by European shamans.

1-56718-370-0, 6 x 9, 288 pp., illus., softcover   **$14.95**

To Order by Phone: 1–800–THE MOON.

Prices subject to change without notice.

HAWAIIAN RELIGION & MAGIC
Scott Cunninham

The religion of the ancient Hawaiians was a rich, all-encompassing
spirituality deeply rooted in the
land, the wind, the rain and the
ocean. This is the first book solely
devoted to the spirituality of the
Hawaiian people and how taboos,
superstitions and magical practices
permeated and defined every
aspect of their lives.

Taking a historical and sociological
perspective, *Traditional Hawaiian
Religion & Magic* examines in
detail the fascinating beliefs of old
Hawaii: the structure of its society
of rulers, commoners and slaves; the names and ways of the many
major and minor deities; the practice of deifying ancestral spirits; the
magical and religious importance of dance, colors, water, stone and
plants; and the underlying concept of *mana*, the Hawaiians' name for
the spiritual power that pervades all things. Cunningham also discuss-
es traditional Hawaiian methods of divination, reading omens, practicing magic and predicting the future, and the extent to which these
traditions live on today. This well-researched book views Hawaiian religious beliefs as a whole rather than serving as a textbook for practicing
modern magic.

1-56718-199-6, 256 pp., 6 x 9, 8 color plates, softcover $12.95

To Order by Phone: 1–800–THE MOON.
Prices subject to change without notice.

DANCE OF POWER
A Shamanic Journey
Dr. Susan Gregg

Join Dr. Susan Gregg on her fascinating, real-life journey to find her soul. This is the story of her shamanic apprenticeship with a man named Miguel, a Mexican-Indian Shaman, or "Nagual." As you live the author's personal experiences, you have the opportunity to take a quantum leap along the path toward personal freedom, toward finding your true self, and grasping the ultimate personal freedom—the freedom to choose moment by moment what you want to experience.

Here, in a warm and genuine style, Dr. Gregg details her studies with Miguel, her travel to other realms, and her initiations by fire and water into the life of a "warrior." If you want to understand how you create your own reality—and how you may be wasting energy by resisting change or trying to understand the unknowable—take the enlightening path of the Nagual. Practical exercises at the end of each chapter give you the tools to embark upon your own spiritual quest.

Learn about another way of being ... *Dance of Power* can change your life, if you let it.

0-87542-247-0, 240 pp., 5 1/4 x 8, illus., photos, softbound $12.95

To Order by Phone: 1–800–THE MOON.

Prices subject to change without notice.

SHAMANISM AND THE MYSTERY LINES

Ley Lines, Spirit Paths, Shape-Shifting & Out-of-Body Travel
Paul Devereux

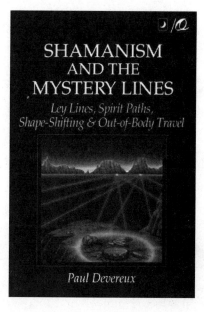

This book will take you across archaic landscapes, into contact with spiritual traditions as old as the human central nervous system and into the deepest recesses of the human psyche. Explore the mystery surrounding "ley lines": stone rows, prehistoric linear earthwork, and straight tracks in archaic landscapes around the world. Why would the ancients, without the wheel or horse, want such broad and exact roads? Why the apparent obsession with straightness? Why the parallel sections?

Are they energy lines? Traders' tracks? For those who have definite ideas as to what a ley line is, be prepared for a surprise . . . and a possible shift in your beliefs about this intriguing phenomenon.

The theory put forth and proved in *Shamanism and the Mystery Lines* is startling: that all ancient landscape lines—whether physical manifestations as created by the Amerindians or conceptual as in the case of Feng shui—are in essence *spirit lines*. And underlying the concept of spirit and straightness is a deep, universal experience yielded by the human central nervous system: that of shamanic magical flight—or the out-of-body experience. This explanation is as simple and direct as the lines themselves . . . flight is the straight way over land.

0-87542-189-X, 240 pp., 6 x 9, illus., softcover   **$12.95**

To Order by Phone: 1–800–THE MOON.
Prices subject to change without notice.

VISIONS OF MURDER
a novel by
Florence Wagner McClain

Set in a scenic Oregon resort town surrounded by mountains and vast natural beauty, this suspense novel delves into the real problems of New Mexico's black market of stolen Indian artifacts. *Visions of Murder* mixes fact-based psychic experiences with lively archeological dialogue in a plot that unravels the high toll this black market exacts in lives, knowledge, and money.

David Manning was gunned down in an execution-style shooting outside his office. Unknown to his wife Janet, David had just discovered evidence in his employer's data bank of money-laundering connected to a black market in Indian artifacts.

Janet embarks on a personally exhaustive investigation into the death of her husband when she unearths a kind of dirt she's not used to handling. Elements of the occult, romance, and murder simmer hotly in this bubbling cauldron of mystery that is as informative as it is absorbing.

1-56718-452-9, 336 pp., mass market, softcover   **$5.99**

To Order by Phone: 1–800–THE MOON.

Prices subject to change without notice.